OUT OF THE BLUE:

THE GIANTS' SHOCKING
SUPER SEASON

DAILY☉NEWS

NYDailyNews.com

Peter J. Clark, Publisher
Molly Voorheis, Managing Editor
Nicky Brillowski, Book and Cover Design
Sam Schmidt, Advertising

ISBN: 978-0-9837337-8-2 (PB)
ISBN: 978-0-9837337-9-9 (HC)

Printed in the United States of America
KCI Sports Publishing   3340 Whiting Avenue, Suite 5   Stevens Point, WI 54481
Phone: 1-800-697-3756   Fax: 715-344-2668
www.kcisports.com

CONTENTS

FOREWARD

BY RALPH VACCHIANO

It was a miracle the first time, when the 2007 Giants came out of the blue and knocked off the undefeated New England Patriots. It was a shocking finish to season that seemed to be going nowhere. A one-in-a-million shot. A once-in-a-lifetime moment.

Now, the New York Giants have done it again.

Lightning struck twice, as the Giants capped another improbable run to an NFL championship, with a 21-17 win over the New England Patriots in Super Bowl XLVI. For the second time in four years, this time under a dome in Indianapolis, they stood on a podium at midfield, clutching the Vince Lombardi Trophy as confetti swirled around them, ready to carry the silver prize down the Canyon of Heroes one more time.

That they won it again against two icons of this era — Bill Belichick and Tom Brady — only added to the greatness of what has become a golden era of Giants football. Tom Coughlin and Eli Manning now have two Super Bowl rings in the last five seasons, securing their place among the greatest Giants coaches and quarterbacks of all time.

And just like in 2007, nobody saw this coming - at least nobody but the Giants themselves. When the team was losing free agents and the bodies started dropping in July and August due to injury, Giants general manager Jerry Reese tried to tell everyone that "We'll get into the playoffs and we'll make a run." Nobody believed him, just like nobody believed Manning when he went on the radio days earlier and insisted he was an elite, Top 5 quarterback who belonged in Tom Brady's class.

Little by little, though, the pieces came together. Manning put together the finest of his eight NFL seasons. The world discovered the magic of Victor Cruz, the second-year sensation who had one of the greatest seasons ever by a Giants receiver and salsa-danced his way onto the national stage. Together, they helped hold the team together despite a four-game losing streak midway through the season that sparked fears of another second-half collapse and left the Giants teetering on the edge at 7-7 with two games to play.

Then the magical run began with a jolt a 99-yard touchdown from Manning to Cruz in a Christmas Eve win over the Jets in the Battle of New York. And with a suddenly healthy and revived defense behind them, the Giants never looked back. They snuck into the playoffs on the final night of the regular season and got on a roll for the ages that included another overtime field goal by Lawrence Tynes to win the NFC Championship Game.

Then, on Feb. 5, 2012, at Lucas Oil Stadium, history repeated itself. Coughlin, Manning and the upstart Giants stared down Belichick, Brady and their New England empire just like they did before.

"It's overwhelming," said Giants safety Antrel Rolle. "Not so much that we're here, but because of what it took to get here. This is well-deserved. It was a long, hard road, and we made it."

Yes they did. They made it from the brink of elimination, all the way to the end of the Canyon of Heroes.

Again. ∎

Right: Tom Coughlin celebrates at the end of the Giants' 21-17 win. *Ron Antonelli | Daily News*

OUT OF THE BLUE.

OUT OF THE BLUE

GAME ONE
REDSKINS 28 | GIANTS 14

AN EMOTIONAL DAY RESULTS IN AN UNACCEPTABLE LOSS FOR BIG BLUE

BY RALPH VACCHIANO

In the eerie quiet of the Giants' locker room last night, the loudest words came from defensive tackle Chris Canty. It was bad enough for him that they lost their opener after a long and miserable summer.

But for a New York team to play like that on the 10th anniversary of the Sept. 11 terrorist attacks, of all days? It was just too much for the Bronx-born Canty to take.

"We don't live in a bubble as professional athletes," Canty said after the Giants opened the regular season with a 28-14 loss to the Redskins. "We know what 9/11 means to us, what it means to our fans, what it means to our city, what it means to this country. We represent the red, white and blue. And to go out there, put that kind of performance out there is unacceptable to us.

"It's unacceptable in every regard."

Unacceptable and unexpected, at least by the Giants, who seemed so sure they'd be able to turn around their summer of doom and gloom as soon as the games started for real. Instead their defense was shredded for 305 yards by Redskins quarterback Rex Grossman, and their own quarterback, Eli Manning, opened the second half by throwing an interception that rookie defensive end Ryan Kerrigan returned for a touchdown.

They were out of sync. They couldn't tackle. They had a field goal blocked. They picked up right where they left off after their sloppy, uninspired preseason.

"We just continued to make the kind of mistakes that Coach (Tom) Coughlin told us not to make," Canty said. "At some point we need to listen."

The Giants knew it wasn't going to be easy with some new faces on offense and without four defensive starters, including defensive end Justin Tuck, who was a late scratch due to continued issues with his neck. They had hoped, though, that the emotion of the day and the pregame ceremony would spark them somehow, or at least get their attention.

Instead they looked flat. Manning, who finished 18-of-32 for 268 yards, opened 0-for-4, and three of those passes bounced off the hands

Left: Giants QB Eli Manning is sacked by Redskins linebacker London Fletcher, left, and nose tackle Chris Neil. *Susan Walsh | AP Photo*

Above: After the Giants jumped out to a 7-0 lead, the Redskins' offensive line manhandled Big Blue's defense all afternoon.
Thomas E. Witte | AP Photo

of his receivers — running back Ahmad Bradshaw, receiver Victor Cruz and tight end Jake Ballard. He did hit a 68-yard pass to Hakeem Nicks and then opened the scoring on a bootleg touchdown run from the Redskins' 2.

But their demise would begin shortly after that, and was on full display in the second half, when they produced just 102 yards. Worse, with the score tied 14-14 on the first series of the third quarter, Manning tried to hit Nicks on a quick screen from the Giants' 18. But Kerrigan avoided the low block attempt from right tackle Kareem McKenzie,

leaped up to deflect the pass, caught it and rumbled nine yards into the end zone.

Coughlin said that was "a tough way to start the second half," but the Giants made it tougher when Bradshaw (13 carries, 44 yards) got stuffed on a fourth-and-1 from the Washington 31 later in the third quarter. Then in the fourth, after a sack and forced fumble by Jason Pierre-Paul got the offense the ball back at the Redskins' 27, the Giants stalled again and settled for a 38-yard field goal attempt by Lawrence Tynes. The kick was blocked, leaving the Giants down a touch-down.

SCORE BY QUARTERS	1	2	3	4	FINAL
Giants	7	7	0	0	14
Washington	0	14	7	7	28

8

OUT OF THE BLUE.

"That was extremely disappointing," Coughlin said. "That very well may have changed the complexion of the game completely there."

It did because Grossman (21-of-34, 305 yards, two touchdowns) was picking apart the Giants' secondary. And, with the help of a big unnecessary roughness penalty on Giants safety Antrel Rolle, Grossman turned that block into a game-sealing, 4-yard touchdown pass to Jabar Gaffney with 5:04 left in the game.

After that, the Giants had no chance. Even Coughlin could see the offense was hopelessly out of sync.

"I did not like the end of our game offensively at all," he said. "We didn't move. We looked disorganized."

That's the way the offense looked all summer, too. Still the Giants all seemed surprised after seeing their six-game winning streak against the Redskins snapped and their three-game winning streak in the opener.

"At this point, that loss stings, it really does," said defensive end Dave Tollefson. "In the division, this early in the season, it stings a lot."

For Canty, and probably some of his teammates as well, it stung for much deeper reasons than that.

"For us, understanding what we represented and to do what we did out there today," Canty said, "it's embarrassing." ∎

Above: Eli Manning leaves the field after a disappointing start to the 2011 season. *Susan Walsh | AP Photo*

SCORING SUMMARY

FIRST QUARTER
GIANTS – Manning 2 run (Tynes kick), 9:53.

SECOND QUARTER
REDSKINS – Hightower 1 run (Gano kick), 11:25.
GIANTS – Bradshaw 6 run (Tynes kick), 2:48.
REDSKINS – Armstrong 6 pass from Grossman (Gano kick), :37.

THIRD QUARTER
REDSKINS – Kerrigan 9 interception return (Gano kick), 13:03.

FOURTH QUARTER
REDSKINS – Gaffney 4 pass from Grossman (Gano kick), 5:04.

SCORING SUMMARY

	GIANTS	WASH
First downs	15	22
Total Net Yards	315	332
Rushes-yards	20-75	26-74
Passing	240	258
Punt Returns	2-27	5-53
Kickoff Returns	2-21	2-48
Interceptions Ret.	0-0	1-9
Comp-Att-Int	18-32-1	21-34-0
Sacked-Yards Lost	4-28	4-47
Punts	6-45.2	6-43.0
Fumbles-Lost	1-0	1-1
Penalties-Yards	8-63	3-25
Time of Possession	27:24	32:36

Attendance — 80,121

INDIVIDUAL STATISTICS

RUSHING
Giants — Bradshaw 13-44, Jacobs 6-29, Manning 1-2.
Washington — Hightower 25-72, Helu 1-2.

PASSING
Giants — Manning 18-32-1-268.
Washington — Grossman 21-34-0-305.

RECEIVING
Giants — Nicks 7-122, Manningham 4-49, Ballard 2-59, Hixon 2-21, Bradshaw 1-10, Hynoski 1-4, Ware 1-3.
Washington — Moss 6-76, Davis 5-105, Gaffney 3-54, Hightower 3-25, Armstrong 2-24, Cooley 2-21.

MISSED FIELD GOALS
Giants — Tynes 38 (BK).
Washington — Gano 39 (WR).

GAME STATS
SEPTEMBER 11, 2011

OUT OF THE BLUE.

GAME TWO
GIANTS 28 | RAMS 16

TAKE THOSE FINGERS OFF THE PANIC BUTTON, THE GIANTS SHOW SIGNS OF LIFE AND EARN THEIR FIRST VICTORY

BY RALPH VACCHIANO

It took a little while for them to get going, and they had to shake off a terrible start by Eli Manning to do it, but after a summer of waiting, the Giants finally got into a bit of a groove. They came up with several big plays, including a huge defensive touchdown from linebacker Michael Boley, as they won their home opener last night, 28-16, over the St. Louis Rams.

It wasn't pretty, and even Tom Coughlin said, "there's much to be improved upon." But with their grudge match in Philly looming just five days from now, at least it was a start.

"It was very important going into this week with Philly," said receiver Hakeem Nicks. "It's a little confidence boost going in with a win under our belt."

For a while, it didn't look as if the Giants would do enough to get that. Manning got off to a miserable, 2-for-11 start, including another interception on the opening drive of the game. Meanwhile, Rams quarterback Sam Bradford, on his way to a career-high 331 yards, was slicing through the Giants' overmatched secondary. The Rams were blistering the Giants

Above: Linebacker Michael Boley scores huge defensive touchdown, helping Giants beat the Rams. *Robert Sabo | Daily News*

Left: Eli Manning drops back to pass against the Rams in what turns out to be a 200-yard, 2-TD afternoon. *Ron Antonelli | Daily News*

with the no-huddle, making things worse for a defense that was already confused.

But the Giants (1-1) turned the tide with a wave of big plays, starting when Rams rookie Greg Salas fumbled a punt return and Big Blue defensive end Dave Tollefson recovered. That led to a sparkling, one-handed, fourth-down catch along the sidelines by Nicks, a play that was actually ruled a no-catch, but the Giants got the ball at the Rams' 9 thanks to a pass-interference penalty.

Two plays later, Nicks made another impressive catch, reaching in front of Rams cornerback Bradley Fletcher for a 3-yard touchdown and a 7-3 Giants lead.

Then it was the defense's turn. Early in the second quarter, with the Rams (0-2) driving and trailing only 7-6, Bradford threw a pass that was dropped by running back Cadillac Williams. But Boley saw that the pass was backward, making the play a fumble. So he alertly grabbed the ball and raced 65 yards for the touchdown and a 14-6 Giants lead.

It was the Giants' first defensive touchdown since cornerback Terrell Thomas scored on an interception against Washington on Dec. 21, 2009, and the Giants never really looked back. Even Manning (18-for-29, 200 yards) got better as the game went, completing 16 of his final 18 passes.

"I think he started seeing things better," Coughlin said. "Early on we had some difficulties, but as we got going we got better."

"We're definitely not playing as well as we need to be at times," Manning added. "But at key moments I thought we made some big plays."

They would continue, too, especially when the Giants turned the tables on Rams coach Steve Spagnuolo, their former defensive coordinator, and turned up the pressure on Bradford. When they did, they gave their own offense time for a couple more big plays at the end of the first half. The first was a bobbling, falling, 31-yard catch by Mario Manningham — a play on which he may have suffered a concussion. The second was a spectacular falling catch by Hixon in the end zone in which he tipped the ball to himself twice with his right hand before making the grab. The 22-yard touchdown catch — on which Hixon injured his right calf — gave the Giants an improbable 21-6 halftime lead.

Remarkably, with Manningham and Hixon out of the game, the Giants still ran some five-receiver sets and put the finishing touches on the game with a 9-yard touchdown run by Brandon Jacobs in the third quarter.

When it was finally over, Coughlin looked more relieved than pleased. He knew his secondary -

Above: Wide receiver Hakeem Nicks poses after scoring a touchdown vs. the Rams. *Robert Sabo* I *Daily News*

from which he benched cornerback Aaron Ross for part of the second half - was terrible for the second straight week. He also wasn't thrilled that the rushing attack produced only 3.1 yards per carry (38 rushes, 119 yards).

"But at some key moments in the game, I thought we stepped up and played well," Manning said. "When they gave us a little opening, we seemed to jump in there and score a touchdown instead of settling for field goals."

And that gave them a much-needed victory, one that briefly lifted their spirits after a summer of despair. It may have been ugly, but nobody was complaining.

"There's no such thing as an ugly win," said defensive end Justin Tuck. "A win's a win."∎

SCORE BY QUARTERS	1	2	3	4	FINAL
St. Louis	6	0	10	0	16
Giants	7	14	7	0	28

OUT OF THE BLUE.

Above: Ahmad Bradshaw tries to break free from St. Louis cornerback Bradley Fletcher. *Ron Antonelli* | *Daily News*

SCORING SUMMARY

FIRST QUARTER
RAMS – FG Jo.Brown 21, 9:14.
GIANTS – Nicks 3 pass from Manning (Tynes kick), 5:47.
RAMS – FG Jo.Brown 25, 3:21.

SECOND QUARTER
GIANTS – Boley 65 fumble return (Tynes kick), 10:58.
GIANTS – Hixon 22 pass from Manning (Tynes kick), :21.

THIRD QUARTER
RAMS – FG Jo.Brown 27, 11:49.
GIANTS – Jacobs 9 run (Tynes kick), 6:19.
RAMS – Alexander 19 pass from Bradford (Jo.Brown kick), 1:18.

SCORING SUMMARY

	STL	GIANTS
First downs	14	22
Total Net Yards	367	300
Rushes-yards	19-59	38-119
Passing	308	181
Punt Returns	2-29	3-17
Kickoff Returns	4-90	2-51
Interceptions Ret.	1-0	0-0
Comp-Att-Int	22-46-0	18-29-1
Sacked-Yards Lost	2-23	3-19
Punts	7-44.7	7-46.0
Fumbles-Lost	4-2	0-0
Penalties-Yards	8-85	5-55
Time of Possession	25:48	34:12

Attendance — 70,741

INDIVIDUAL STATISTICS

RUSHING
St. Louis — C.Williams 13-36, Bradford 3-15, Norwood 3-8.
Giants — Bradshaw 15-59, Jacobs 16-50, Ware 3-22, Manning 4-(minus 12).

PASSING
St. Louis — Bradford 22-46-0-331.
Giants — Manning 18-29-1-200.

RECEIVING
St. Louis — Sims-Walker 6-92, B.Gibson 4-52, Salas 4-27, Alexander 3-122, C.Williams 3-4, Kendricks 1-26, Hoomanawanui 1-8.
Giants — Bradshaw 5-45, Manningham 3-56, Nicks 3-15, Hixon 2-29, Cruz 2-17, Jacobs 1-17, Ballard 1-13, Hynoski 1-8.

GAME STATS
SEPTEMBER 19, 2011

OUT OF THE BLUE.

GAME THREE
GIANTS 29 | EAGLES 16

IT WASN'T A DREAM, IT REALLY HAPPENED

BY RALPH VACCHIANO

And the Giants weren't the least bit surprised.

Undermanned and under-appreciated, the Giants did yesterday what so many thought would be impossible, and afterward they insisted they never had a doubt. They stunned the Philadelphia Eagles, 29-16, at Lincoln Financial Field, and dropped the self-appointed "Dream Team" to the bottom of the NFC East.

"They call them the Dream Team, but they've got a lot to prove to be that," said running back Ahmad Bradshaw. "We knew we were better than them."

They might have been the only ones, considering how banged up they've been since the season started. But they got a huge game from some of their replace-

Above: Wide receiver Victor Cruz (80) celebrates a touchdown with teammate Henry Hynoski (45). *Corey Sipkin | Daily News*

Left: Running back Ahmad Bradshaw (44) fights off the Philadelphia defense. *Corey Sipkin | Daily News*

ments, including receiver Victor Cruz and cornerback Aaron Ross. Cruz, the second-year pro who filled in for the injured Mario Manningham, caught three passes for 110 yards and two touchdowns. Ross, in for the injured Terrell Thomas and fresh off a benching last week, had two interceptions.

The Giants, who snapped a six-game losing streak to the Eagles, also got a four-touchdown game from Eli Manning, 139 combined yards from Ahmad Bradshaw and a punishing performance from a defense that battered Eagles quarterback Michael Vick and chased him with a broken right hand in the fourth quarter.

It wasn't enough to erase the memory of their brutal collapse against the Eagles last December. But considering they staged their own comeback after blowing an early 14-0 lead, they're hoping this win gives them a much-needed emotional spark.

"They took the lead and I would bet no one in this locker room thought about last year," said guard Chris Snee. "I think the confidence in this locker room just went a lot higher."

The Giants (2-1) played with confidence early, especially when Ross ended the Eagles' first drive by picking off a pass from Vick (16-for-23, 176 yards, one interception) that bounced off former Giants receiver Steve Smith. The Giants turned that into a 40-yard play-action pass from Manning (16-for-23, 254 yards, four touchdowns) to running back Brandon Jacobs and a 7-0 lead.

One drive later, they got a remarkable 74-yard touchdown catch by Cruz, who bounced off Eagles safety Kurt Coleman and made cornerback Nnamdi Asomougha miss. When the two defensive backs collided behind him, Cruz was gone down the sidelines and the Giants were up 14-0.

But the Eagles (1-2), behind LeSean McCoy's 128 rushing yards, came back, pulling within 14-13 at the half and taking a 16-14 lead on Alex Henery's 21-yard field goal late in the third quarter — after a brilliant four-play goal-line stand by the Giants kept the Eagles out of the end zone. The Eagles even had a chance to make that loom large by pinning the Giants deep in their own territory with a punt on a fourth-and-1 from the Giants' 43 with 11:43 to play.

Instead, Eagles coach Andy Reid ordered the Eagles to go for it — a decision many Giants took as a slap in the face.

"I think what happens there is they're confident that they either have a play or something they're very, very sure is going to be effective," said Tom Coughlin. "We thought very well about what we were doing as well."

The Giants turned out to be right as linebacker Michael Boley stopped McCoy for a three-yard loss. Seven plays later, Cruz leaped at the goal line in double coverage and pulled down a 28-yard touchdown catch that, after a two-point conversion, put the Giants up 22-16.

That fourth-down play turned out to be Vick's last. He had broken his right hand in the third quarter and tried to play through it, but couldn't continue. When Mike Kafka replaced him after the Giants' touchdown, he was picked off on his first pass by Ross with eight minutes left in the game.

The Giants turned that into a touchdown, too — with the help of the Eagles being lured into an offsides penalty on Lawrence Tynes' field goal attempt that kept that drive alive.

Above: Tom Coughlin encourages his team.
Corey Sipkin | Daily News

Above: Cornerback Aaron Ross grabs an interception.
Corey Sipkin | Daily News

SCORE BY QUARTERS	1	2	3	4	FINAL
Giants	14	0	0	15	29
Philadelphia	0	13	3	0	16

OUT OF THE BLUE.

Above: Brandon Jacobs bulldozes his way for a two-point conversion in the fourth quarter. *Corey Sipkin | Daily News*

And when Bradshaw took a short pass from Manning and scampered into the end zone with 3:32 left, the celebration on the sidelines was on.

It was cathartic for the Giants, and not just because of the emotional baggage they carried from last Dec. 19, when they blew a 31-10 lead at home to the Eagles and lost 38-31.

Yes, it was a chance to finish what they started. But it was also a chance to silence all the "Dream Team" nonsense they've been hearing from Philadelphia since the summer began.

"They can continue to be the Dream Team," running back Brandon Jacobs said, "and keep dreaming." ■

SCORING SUMMARY

FIRST QUARTER
GIANTS – Jacobs 40 pass from Manning (Tynes kick), 6:04.
GIANTS – Cruz 74 pass from Manning (Tynes kick), :49.

SECOND QUARTER
EAGLES – FG Henery 21, 7:47.
EAGLES – McCoy 11 run (Henery kick), 1:54.
EAGLES – FG Henery 38, :00.

THIRD QUARTER
EAGLES – FG Henery 21, :59.

FOURTH QUARTER
GIANTS – Cruz 28 pass from Manning (Jacobs run), 8:07.
GIANTS – Bradshaw 18 pass from Manning (Tynes kick), 3:32.

SCORING SUMMARY

	GIANTS	PHI
First downs	14	25
Total Net Yards	334	376
Rushes-yards	25-102	40-177
Passing	232	199
Punt Returns	0-0	1-13
Kickoff Returns	1-33	2-45
Interceptions Ret.	3-32	0-0
Comp-Att-Int	16-23-0	20-30-3
Sacked-Yards Lost	3-22	2-12
Punts	4-41.0	2-45.0
Fumbles-Lost	0-0	3-0
Penalties-Yards	4-21	7-36
Time of Possession	23:09	36:51

Attendance — 69,144

INDIVIDUAL STATISTICS

RUSHING
Giants — Bradshaw 15-86, Jacobs 7-19, Manning 3-[minus 3].
Philadelphia — McCoy 24-128, Vick 7-31, Schmitt 4-6, Brown 3-6, D.Jackson 1-3, Lewis 1-3.

PASSING
Giants — Manning 16-23-0-254.
Philadelphia — Vick 16-23-1-176, Kafka 4-7-2-35.

RECEIVING
Giants — Bradshaw 5-53, Cruz 3-110, Nicks 3-25, Jacobs 2-42, Ballard 1-15, Stokley 1-7, Beckum 1-2.
Philadelphia — Maclin 5-69, Avant 4-33, McCoy 3-13, D.Jackson 2-30, Smith 2-27, Celek 2-9, Harbor 1-17, Schmitt 1-13.

GAME STATS
SEPTEMBER 25, 2011

OUT OF THE BLUE.

GAME FOUR
GIANTS 31 | CARDINALS 27

CRUZ CATCHES A BREAK

BY RALPH VACCHIANO

Victor Cruz wasn't entirely sure what happened, but he still exhaled more deeply than he ever had before. He was "a little scared" that he had just fumbled away a Giants comeback.

He wasn't the only one.

The entire Giants organization held its breath until the officials ruled that Cruz's apparent fourth-quarter fumble wasn't a fumble and also wasn't reviewable. Knowing they may have caught a break, the Giants pounced and one play later, Eli Manning hit Hakeem Nicks for a 29-yard touchdown that capped a wild, fourth-quarter comeback and a 31-27 win over the Arizona Cardinals yesterday.

The Giants scored 21 points in the fourth quarter, 14 in the final 3:37 and erased a 10-point deficit in the final 5:16 to win their third straight game. They did it mostly by riding the red-hot arm of Manning, who completed 27 of 40 passes for 321 yards — including 10 for 162 yards to Nicks.

It was the 17th time Manning has led the Giants back from a fourth-quarter deficit to a win. And he did it by completing 14 of 17 passes for 180 yards and two touchdowns in the fourth at the same site and in the same direction where he made his greatest comeback ever — to win Super Bowl XLII.

But it all nearly ended with 2:46 remaining when Cruz caught a 19-yard pass, fell down and then got up — without the ball.

"I was a little scared, to be honest with you," Cruz said afterward. "Looking at the replay, it looks like somebody touched me, then it looked like they didn't. You never know. Those plays can

Left: Giants' defenders line up against the Arizona Cardinals.
Paul Connors | AP Photo

THE GIANTS' SHOCKING SUPER SEASON

go either way. So I was a little scared."

He had good reason, because after first being tripped by Cards cornerback Michael Adams, Cruz took a few more steps before he fell. He got up and left the ball behind because, he said, "I thought I was touched."

But he wasn't, so Arizona cornerback Richard Marshall picked up the loose football. Then the officials whistled the play dead.

Arizona coach Ken Whisenhunt tried to challenge, but referee Jerome Boger announced that Cruz "gave himself up" and therefore the play was not reviewable. The rule (Rule 7, Section 2, Article 1) says, "an official shall declare the ball dead . . . when a runner . . . declares himself down by falling to the ground . . . and making no effort to advance."

An NFL spokesman, via Twitter, said "it's in judgment-call category," though on Fox, Mike Pereira, the NFL's former director of officiating, indicated Boger's judgment was wrong.

"Yeah, I thought we got a break on that one," Manning said. "I thought it was going to be ruled a fumble. I saw it pretty clear. That's why I tried to get the ball snapped real quick."

Above: Cornerback Corey Webster tackles Arizona wide receiver Larry Fitzgerald, who had a 100-yard receiving game. *Paul Connors* | *AP Photo*

Cardinals safety Kerry Rhodes said the call was "crazy." Whisenhunt wasn't happy, but said, "I'd like to think that it shouldn't have come to that point."

Giants GM Jerry Reese agreed, saying, "I'm not sure what the rule is, but our players did make some plays in the game. That wasn't the only thing that helped us win the game."

He's right. The Giants made many plays after a terrible first three quarters, in which two big turnovers — fumbles by Ahmad Bradshaw and Manning — led to 10 easy points for Arizona and put the Giants in a 20-10 hole. For most of the game, the Giants' offense was erratic, and the defense had no

SCORE BY QUARTERS	1	2	3	4	FINAL
Giants	0	10	0	21	31
Arizona	3	3	14	7	27

OUT OF THE BLUE.

answer for Cards receiver Larry Fitzgerald (eight catches, 102 yards) or running back Beanie Wells (27 carries, 138 yards, three touchdowns).

Even after a Brandon Jacobs touchdown and Antrel Rolle interception in the fourth quarter, the Giants were still down 10 and seemingly finished when Wells scored his third touchdown with 5:17 left in the game.

But magic seems to happen for the Giants here, especially in the northwest end of University of Phoenix stadium. Running the no-huddle to perfection in that direction, Manning first led the Giants to an outstanding 2-yard touchdown catch by tight end Jake Ballard with 3:37 remaining. Then, 27 seconds later, he got the ball back again near midfield for one last game-winning drive.

"You know," Manning said, "we've had some good games here."

Some huge breaks, too. And while this wasn't quite David Tyree pinning a Hail Mary pass against his helmet, it was still remarkable.

"For a long time it was an absolute struggle," Tom Coughlin said. "We just kept playing. We hung in there. We found a way to finish."

"We never forgot what type of team we've got," added receiver Mario Manningham. "We never stopped believing."

Cruz, however, did stop breathing for a moment while the officials made their fateful noncall.

"God was on our side on that one," Nicks said. Good thing for Cruz the referee was, too.■

Above: Wide receiver Hakeem Nicks crosses the goal line with the game-winning touchdown with 2:39 left in the fourth quarter. *Paul Connors | AP Photo*

SCORING SUMMARY

FIRST QUARTER
CARDINALS – FG Feely 27, 13:02.

SECOND QUARTER
CARDINALS – FG Feely 27, 7:57.
GIANTS – Bradshaw 13 run (Tynes kick), 2:54.
GIANTS – FG Tynes 30, :01.

THIRD QUARTER
CARDINALS – Wells 1 run (Feely kick), 10:24.
CARDINALS – Wells 1 run (Feely kick), 2:55.

FOURTH QUARTER
GIANTS – Jacobs 1 run (Tynes kick), 12:07.
CARDINALS – Wells 2 run (Feely kick), 5:16.
GIANTS – Ballard 2 pass from Manning
    (Tynes kick), 3:37.
GIANTS – Nicks 29 pass from Manning
    (Tynes kick), 2:39.

SCORING SUMMARY

	GIANTS	ARI
First downs	24	22
Total Net Yards	360	368
Rushes-yards	24-54	32-156
Passing	306	212
Punt Returns	3-30	3-28
Kickoff Returns	5-120	3-74
Interceptions Ret.	1-0	0-0
Comp-Att-Int	27-40-0	20-34-1
Sacked-Yards Lost	1-15	4-25
Punts	5-44.6	4-45.0
Fumbles-Lost	2-2	2-1
Penalties-Yards	7-55	11-118
Time of Possession	28:01	31:59

Attendance — 60,496

INDIVIDUAL STATISTICS

RUSHING
Giants — Bradshaw 12-39, Jacobs 9-18,
    Manning 3-(minus 3).
Arizona — Wells 27-138, Smith 2-16,
    Kolb 2-1, Stephens-Howling 1-1.

PASSING
Giants — Manning 27-40-0-321.
Arizona — Kolb 20-34-1-237.

RECEIVING
Giants — Nicks 10-162, Cruz 6-98,
    Bradshaw 4-11, Ballard 3-33,
    Manningham 1-10, Hynoski 1-5, Ware 1-2,
    Jacobs 1-0.
Arizona — Fitzgerald 8-102, Heap 4-41,
    Doucet 3-42, Sherman 2-24, Housler 1-16,
    Stephens-Howling 1-9, King 1-3.

GAME STATS
OCTOBER 2, 2011

VICTOR CRUZ

BY RALPH VACCHIANO

Numbers were never going to define Victor Cruz. He was always sure of that, from the day he started learning to play football. It was never about how many passes he caught. It was how he caught them.

His life would not be about statistics, although four years ago, Cruz found himself on the verge of becoming one. Cruz had survived growing up in the rough Fourth Ward in Paterson, N.J., using sports as his way to avoid the gangs and skirt the drug dealers. He proudly walked a high wire above the danger, earning a scholarship on his way to a better life.

In the spring of 2007, it all almost slipped away. The scholarship Cruz had worked so hard for was gone, after he was kicked out of the University of Massachusetts for the second time in a year. He was at home taking online courses, trying to reboot his life when he got a frantic phone call from his older brother telling him their father had died suddenly. "Man, there was a thin line there where this thing could've easily went the other way," the 24-year-old Cruz says now. "I could be home right now, working at the bank or something, thinking 'Man, if I would've done this differently, my life would be a little different.' I was looking at myself, trying to figure out who I was and what I was trying to do with my life. I didn't want to become another stereotype or statistic."

"How do you react?" asks Benjie Wimberly, Cruz's old football coach at now-defunct Paterson Catholic High School, and a family friend. "Tank it, put your head down and say 'I quit. My dad died. Everything around me points to me just being another statistic like everybody else? Or do I really turn my game and life on and move forward?'"

That was long before Cruz unexpectedly rocketed to stardom as a breakout receiver — and crowd favorite - with his hometown Giants. He was just another good athlete in the inner city then. The son of a Puerto Rican mother (Blanca Cruz) and African-American father (Mike Walker), he also wasn't immune to the temptations of the Fourth Ward. "I had my times where I would rebel and would be out and about," Cruz says.

His father was a fireman at the Riverside Station, always wandering the area making sure his son stayed out of trouble. He told Victor that sports were his salvation, his ticket out. The father was the one who lured Cruz from baseball, basketball and karate and introduced him to football. By the time Cruz got to high school, he was a star.

As a 160-pound receiver (and sometimes cornerback), Cruz's size was an issue no matter how many yards and touchdowns he racked up. College recruiters deemed him too small. The closest he came to a Division I scholarship, Wimberly recalls, was when Rutgers considered giving him its last

Above: Victor Cruz salutes the crowd during his breakout season. *Andrew Theodorakis | Daily News*

one in 2005. Instead, the school gave it to Devin McCourty, now a cornerback with the Patriots. Wimberly told Rutgers coach Greg Schiano what he told all the college recruiters: "You're making a mistake. You're missing on this one."

So off Cruz went to Division I-AA UMass, after a brief stop at Brighton Academy in Maine to boost his grades. His stay in Amherst seemed destined to be short. "It was like he was in college, but without the school part," says UMass coach Kevin Morris, then the offensive coordinator. "He was enjoying everything college had to offer except the classes."

Cruz was kicked out of school in the spring of 2006 with a GPA well below 2.0. He returned in the fall, but his grades weren't much better, and he was thrown out again in the spring of 2007 — this time, many thought, for good. Cruz says he wasn't talking much to his dad back then. A year earlier, his father was injured in a car accident,

OUT OF THE BLUE.

Above: Victor Cruz leaps to make a catch in between two Seahawks receivers. *Ron Antonelli | Daily News*

Below: Cruz, who grew up in Paterson, N.J., went from spending most of the 2010 season on injured reserve to Super Bowl champion. *Ron Antonelli | Daily News*

lost his job with the fire department and ended up suing the city for discrimination. Mike Walker seemed depressed after that and, according to family friends, was never the same. Cruz is reluctant to talk about his father's death, but he has said before that he believes his dad committed suicide on March 1, 2007. Whatever happened, Mike Walker's death stung his struggling son, who had suddenly lost one of his biggest supporters while he was still looking for a direction for himself. "It just kind of added a lot of insult to my injury," Cruz says. "It took a big hit on me."

It did something else, too. Wimberly saw the sadness in the kid who "always seemed to tinker along the rules," but he also saw a new spark. "He always had that little edge, like 'I got this. I'm going to make it,' " Wimberly says. "That little bit of swagger, you know?"

Cruz, with his mom's help, begged for another chance at UMass, sitting for a stern lecture over several hours from an associate dean. Cruz returned to UMass for the start of the 2007 season, but slipped one more time - he was hit with a five-game suspension for breaking unspecified team rules. Still, something seemed to finally click. "It was like the light bulb went on and he said, 'This is important to me,' " Morris says. "It was just a matter of focus and maturity. Once the light bulb went on, he went on a roll."

Soon, on the field, Morris saw in Cruz what he calls "that playground sense for getting open."

NFL scouts were flocking to UMass to see offensive lineman Vladimir Ducasse, who would get drafted by the Jets in the second round in 2010. Morris kept pointing them toward the little receiver and implored them to "give that guy a chance."

The Giants did, as an undrafted free agent. Said Giants receivers coach Sean Ryan: "Certain guys have a knack for being able to go and get the ball. I think you could see a little bit of that from Day 1."

The sudden success has changed Victor Cruz's life, but it hasn't changed the kid from the inner city. Wimberly, now a Paterson City Councilman, asks him to return home often and Cruz always does. "I try and be visible so kids can talk to me and shake my hand and know I come from where they come from," Cruz says. "I'm not this big special guy that came from somewhere far away. I walked these same streets as a kid."

A few weeks ago, Cruz was invited to give a pregame talk to the football team at Paterson East Side High School. He arrived early, without an entourage, slipped in unnoticed, and when he was finally introduced to the kids, they went wild. To them, he's a superstar - everything they want to be. To Wimberly, he's "the picture of inner-city perseverance."

That's what Cruz told the kids that day, too, that he was once nearly a statistic before he "came out the other end." "Hey," he said to the kids who looked so familiar, "I'm just like you."■

OUT OF THE BLUE

GAME FIVE
SEAHAWKS 36 | GIANTS 25

BIG BLUE COUGHS IT UP FIVE TIMES IN DEVASTATING LOSS TO SEAHAWKS

BY RALPH VACCHIANO

When the Giants came back and took their fourth-quarter lead, their stadium was rocking and they were dancing. They felt they were in a groove and finally in control of the game.

They never imagined what was about to happen in the final five minutes.

"We fully expected to win," Tom Coughlin said. "About as miserable a feeling as we've had around here in a long time."

It may not have been as heart-breaking, dramatic or even as big as their collapse at home against the Eagles last December, but the shocked look on the Giants' faces after yesterday's 36-25 loss at MetLife Stadium sure seemed eerily similar. They coughed up what they thought would be their fourth straight win by giving up two touchdowns to Seattle in the final 2:37.

The final one was a dagger. The Giants (3-2) trailed by four, but had the ball on the Seattle 10-yard line, seemingly poised to steal another victory in the final minute. Instead, Eli Manning's pass tipped off the hands of near-hero Victor Cruz, ricocheted off Seahawks safety Kam Chancellor and fell into the arms of cornerback Brandon Browner, who returned it 94 yards for a touchdown that sealed the Seahawks' shocking victory.

It was a wild and sloppy game that included eight turnovers — five by the Giants — including three interceptions and a fumble by Manning and a fourth-quarter fumble by Cruz.

The loss wasted a 420-yard, three-touchdown performance by Manning, and another remarkable performance by Cruz, who caught eight passes for 161 yards, including a one-handed grab of a tipped ball that turned into a 68-yard touchdown.

The Giants' turnovers only led to 10 Seattle points, but they completely disrupted their offensive rhythm.

"You can't just play mediocre," Manning said. "You can't make mistakes. They hurt you."

"We played poorly," Coughlin added. "(When) you don't deserve to win, you don't win."

They had their chances, even though the Giants' defense had trouble with the Seahawks' no-huddle offense no matter which quarter-

Left: Giants defensive end Jason Pierre-Paul (90) tackles Seattle Seahawks running back Marshawn Lynch (24) in the 1st half. *Ron Antonelli | Daily News*

back was playing. Tarvaris Jackson carved them up for 166 yards on 15-of-22 passing before injuring his hip in the third quarter. Then Charlie Whitehurst completed 11 of 19 for 149 yards in the second half.

The Seahawks — who had lost nine straight games in the Eastern time zone before yesterday — had only a narrow 19-14 lead, though, thanks to a third-quarter safety when defensive end Anthony Hargrove hammered Giants running back D.J. Ware in the end zone and a 51-yard field goal by Steven Hauschka early in the fourth. That's when the Giants got a magical play from Cruz that seemed to turn the game around.

On a third-and-13 on the Giants' 32, Chancellor read a Manning pass perfectly and jumped in front of Cruz to deflect the ball. But Cruz, off balance, reached out with his right hand, tipped the ball back to himself and made a one-handed catch. Then he took off for a 68-yard touchdown that, after a two-point conversion, put the Giants up 22-19.

The Giants were celebrating, smiling and high-fiving on the field and the sidelines. They felt like the game had completely turned around.

"Yeah, we were ready to go," defensive end Mathias Kiwanuka said. "We had a full head of steam going. We come off of a big play, guys are stepping up. We have to be able to go out and seal the deal."

Instead, they blew it. Cruz fumbled on the Giants' next series deep in Giants territory, giving the Seahawks an easy shot at the tying field goal. Then, after the Giants retook the lead, 25-22, on a 26-yard field goal by Lawrence Tynes, the Seahawks ripped right through the Giants' defense again.

The killer play even featured a mysterious whistle that only the Giants seemed to hear. Before the play, defensive end Osi Umenyiora jumped offsides and several players stopped, thinking they heard a whistle and assuming the play was over. But it wasn't. And when cornerback Aaron Ross and safety Antrel Rolle both tried to cover receiver Ben Obomanu, Doug Baldwin (8 catches, 136 yards) broke free for an easy, 27-yard touchdown catch that put Seattle up 29-25 with 2:37 to go.

"We thought we heard a whistle," Umenyiora said. "But regardless, you can't stop playing, no matter what."

Manning didn't stop. Running his own no-huddle to perfection, he quickly moved the Giants right back

down the field where, with 1:27 remaining, they were at the Seahawks' 5. A false start penalty on left tackle Will Beatty pushed them back to the 10.

Then Manning tried to hit Cruz, who slipped as he tried to cut, got one hand on the ball, but couldn't keep it under control.

"I thought I gripped it," Cruz said. "But as soon as I went to grip it in I got hit and it got bobbled up in the air.

"I knew it was all downhill from there."∎

Score by Quarters	1	2	3	4	Final
Seattle	14	0	2	20	36
Giants	7	7	0	11	25

OUT OF THE BLUE.

Above: Giants defensive end Jason Pierre-Paul sacks Seattle quarterback Tarvaris Jackson in the first half of the Seahawks' victory. *Robert Sabo* I *Daily News*

SCORING SUMMARY

FIRST QUARTER
SEAHAWKS – Obomanu 11 pass from Jackson (Hauschka kick), 12:28.
GIANTS – Ballard 12 pass from Manning (Tynes kick), 9:08.
SEAHAWKS – Lynch 1 run (Hauschka kick), 3:00.

SECOND QUARTER
GIANTS – Nicks 19 pass from Manning (Tynes kick), :11.

THIRD QUARTER
SEAHAWKS – Hargrove safety, 7:02.

FOURTH QUARTER
SEAHAWKS – FG Hauschka 51, 14:28.
GIANTS – Cruz 68 pass from Manning (Bradshaw run), 12:37.
SEAHAWKS – FG Hauschka 43, 10:15.
GIANTS – FG Tynes 26, 4:49.

FOURTH QUARTER (cont.)
SEAHAWKS – Baldwin 27 pass from Whitehurst (Hauschka kick), 2:37.
SEAHAWKS – Browner 94 interception return (Hauschka kick), 1:08.

SCORING SUMMARY

	SEA	GIANTS
First downs	22	21
Total Net Yards	424	464
Rushes-yards	29-145	25-69
Passing	279	395
Punt Returns	6-69	2-12
Kickoff Returns	3-71	3-82
Interceptions Ret.	3-111	1-0
Comp-Att-Int	26-41-1	24-39-3
Sacked-Yards Lost	6-36	3-25
Punts	7-44.6	7-49.0
Fumbles-Lost	3-2	3-2
Penalties-Yards	10-70	7-52
Time of Possession	28:46	31:14

Attendance — 78,650

INDIVIDUAL STATISTICS

RUSHING
Seattle — Lynch 12-98, Jackson 4-17, Washington 3-10, Forsett 4-9, Whitehurst 2-6, Robinson 3-5, Rice 1-0.
Giants — Bradshaw 17-58, Manning 3-5, Ware 4-3, Cruz 1-3.

PASSING
Seattle — Jackson 15-22-1-166, Whitehurst 11-19-0-149.
Giants — Manning 24-39-3-420.

RECEIVING
Seattle — Baldwin 8-136, Obomanu 6-51, Rice 4-38, Lynch 4-33, Tate 2-31, A.McCoy 1-20, Washington 1-6.
Giants — Cruz 8-161, Manningham 5-56, Nicks 4-65, Ballard 3-72, Bradshaw 2-27, Ware 1-22, Pascoe 1-17.

GAME STATS
OCTOBER 9, 2011

OUT OF THE BLUE.

GAME SIX
GIANTS 27 | BILLS 24

BIG BLUE OVERCOMES TWO HUGE FIRST-QUARTER TOUCHDOWNS TO AVOID DEVASTATING HOME LOSS

BY RALPH VACCHIANO

Justin Tuck has seen teams disintegrate from the sidelines, and he knows it could have happened yesterday to the Giants. Two huge first-quarter plays by the Buffalo Bills could've easily sent them spiraling out of control.

Instead, outside of the impassioned pleas of safety Antrel Rolle, Tuck saw his teammates stay mostly calm in the rough early going. He could tell they believed they'd find a way to turn the game around.

"No one panics," Tuck said. "I've been on that sideline sometimes where it just seems that everything is in disarray. Guys just stepped up and played ball."

They did that and more in the fourth quarter, starting when cornerback Corey Webster jumped in front of Bills receiver Steve Johnson at the 4-yard line with 4:02 remaining and grabbed his second interception of the game. That turned what could've been a game-winning drive for Buffalo into an opportunity for the Giants.

Nine plays later, they made the Bills pay with a 23-yard Lawrence Tynes field goal with 1:32 remaining that sealed the Giants' 27-24 win at MetLife Stadium.

It was a huge statement win for the Giants (4-2), who went from being on the brink of taking a two-game losing streak into the bye week to sitting in first place in the NFC East. They didn't commit a single turnover against the most turnover-happy team in the league. They got 122 yards from their struggling running game, including a big 30-yarder by Ahmad Bradshaw (104 yards, three touchdowns) on the final drive. They even sacked Bills quarterback Ryan Fitzpatrick three times — the same number of sacks he had suffered in the first five games of the season.

Most importantly, though, they got a huge bounce-back performance by a defense that allowed an 80-yard touchdown run to Fred Jackson and a 60-yard touchdown pass from Fitzpatrick to Naaman Roosevelt in the first quarter. The much-maligned defense settled down after that, giving up just 196 yards the rest of the game.

Left: Ahmad Bradshaw rushes for 104 yards and three touchdowns to help the Giants hold off Buffalo. *Ron Antonelli | Daily News*

"That's why we're brothers," Rolle said. "We could've started going against each other, but we didn't. We stuck together as a team, and it paid off for us at the end of the day."

Webster was the hero with two outstanding interceptions in the second half, including one down the sidelines about which Tom Coughlin said, "It's going to be hard to believe he even saw that ball." Webster said he knew that after giving up those two early big plays, the defense "needed to make a couple of stops to make up for those."

It started, according to Tuck, with Rolle using some unprintable words toward his defensive teammates on the sidelines, apparently for some much-needed encouragement. Their tackling on the two big plays was indefensible. On the Jackson run, the defensive line was blown off the line of scrimmage and safety Deon Grant whiffed in the open field. On the Roosevelt touchdown, linebacker Michael Boley was late in coverage and then Webster and cornerback Justin Tryon let him slip by.

"We did a good job of just calming down," Tuck said. "Those two big plays were just simple errors - a missed tackle here, a guy minding his gap here. There wasn't a lot of coaching needed there."

"At the end of the day we couldn't let those two plays determine the outcome of the game," Rolle added. "And we didn't."

At first the credit for that went to Eli Manning (21-of-32, 292 yards) and Bradshaw, who kept the Giants in the game. Bradshaw had two 1-yard touchdown runs in the 17-17 first half, and he added another midway through the third quarter to give the Giants a 24-17 lead.

That's when things seemed to tilt the Bills' way again. First, what appeared to be a 37-yard touchdown pass from Manning to Mario Manningham was ruled incomplete by the officials (and upheld after a too-close-to-call video replay). Then Coughlin

Above: Wide receiver Hakeem Nicks hauls in a long-yardage catch. *Robert Sabo | Daily News*

added to what he called "the drama" when he sent out Tynes for a 51-yard field goal that the Bills blocked.

The Bills turned that block into a 9-yard touchdown pass to Johnson that tied the game at 24-24 with 8:57 remaining. Then they got the ball back again with 6:49 to go and were well on their way to the go-ahead score.

That's when the defense stepped up and Webster came up with the second of what Coughlin called "two super plays." Rolle called them "exceptional." Tuck called them "timely." And after Tynes kicked his field goal and the defense had one last stand, they also turned out to be enough for the win.

"We didn't start off well early on in the game, giving them two big plays," Webster said. "But other than that we just kept fighting."

"We weren't doing much right," added Boley. "I'm glad to see we were able to bounce back."∎

SCORE BY QUARTERS	1	2	3	4	FINAL
Buffalo	14	3	0	7	24
Giants	7	10	7	3	27

OUT OF THE BLUE.

Above: Ahmad Bradshaw flexes his muscles after scoring one of his three touchdowns on the day.
Robert Sabo | Daily News

SCORING SUMMARY

FIRST QUARTER
GIANTS – Bradshaw 1 run (Tynes kick), 5:20.
BILLS – Jackson 80 run (Lindell kick), 5:06.
BILLS – Roosevelt 60 pass from Fitzpatrick
　　　　(Lindell kick), :24.

SECOND QUARTER
GIANTS – FG Tynes 26, 9:51.
GIANTS – Bradshaw 1 run (Tynes kick), 2:58.
BILLS – FG Lindell 49, :39.

THIRD QUARTER
GIANTS – Bradshaw 1 run (Tynes kick), 6:53.

FOURTH QUARTER
BILLS – St.Johnson 9 pass from Fitzpatrick
　　　　(Lindell kick), 8:57.
GIANTS – FG Tynes 23, 1:32.

SCORING SUMMARY

	BUF	GIANTS
First downs	17	24
Total Net Yards	374	414
Rushes-yards	23-155	33-122
Passing	219	292
Punt Returns	2-11	1-17
Kickoff Returns	1-21	4-88
Interceptions Ret.	0-0	2-25
Comp-Att-Int	21-30-2	21-32-0
Sacked-Yards Lost	3-25	0-0
Punts	3-45.3	3-53.7
Fumbles-Lost	1-0	0-0
Penalties-Yards	7-75	7-79
Time of Possession	29:13	30:47

Attendance — 79,243

INDIVIDUAL STATISTICS

RUSHING
Buffalo — Jackson 16-121, B.Smith 4-26,
　Fitzpatrick 3-8.
Giants — Bradshaw 26-104, Ware 5-19,
　Manning 2-[minus 1].

PASSING
Buffalo — Fitzpatrick 21-30-2-244.
Giants — Manning 21-32-0-292. .

RECEIVING
Buffalo — Jackson 5-47, St.Johnson 5-39,
　Spiller 5-39, Nelson 4-62, Roosevelt 1-60,
　Chandler 1-[minus 3].
Giants — Ballard 5-81, Manningham 5-56,
　Nicks 4-96, Bradshaw 2-26, Pascoe 2-17,
　Cruz 2-12, Scott 1-4.

MISSED FIELD GOALS
Giants — Tynes 50 [BK].

GAME STATS
OCTOBER 16, 2011

OUT OF THE BLUE.

GAME SEVEN
GIANTS 20 | DOLPHINS 17

THE GIANTS WEREN'T WORRIED, MANNING WOULD BAIL THEM OUT

BY RALPH VACCHIANO

The Giants had done a great job of embarrassing themselves through the first three quarters Sunday and were on the brink of one of the worst home losses in a history filled with some big ones.

They weren't worried at all, though. They knew somehow, some way, Eli Manning would bail them out.

It should never have come to that, of course, but it did, and for the 18th time in his career, Manning turned a fourth-quarter deficit into a victory. He capped a 349-yard day with a 25-yard touchdown pass to Victor Cruz with 5:58 remaining to give the Giants a much-needed, harder-than-it-should-have-been 20-17 victory.

The fact that it came against a winless Miami Dolphins team made it less a cause for celebration, and more a reason to breathe a big sigh of relief.

"I'm starting to see gray hairs," said defensive end Justin Tuck. "But we have the utmost confidence in Eli and his guys. He's playing awesome. He told you all at the beginning of the year that he was elite. I feel like he's proving it right now."

Manning was outstanding yesterday, completing 31 of 45 passes for 349 yards and two touchdowns at MetLife Stadium. The rest of the Giants (5-2)? Not so much. Manning's day would've been even better if it weren't for at least four drops by his running backs, tight ends and receivers.

And the Giants' defense, for 3½ quarters, had no answers for Dolphins quarterback Matt Moore (138 passing yards, 31 rushing) and running back Reggie Bush (103 rushing yards). In fact, in a span of 9½ minutes in the first half, the Giants gave up back-to-back touchdowns to the Dolphins (0-7) — the first touchdowns the Dolphins had scored on consecutive drives all year.

The Giants trailed 14-10 at halftime, and they were only that close because Manning ran a brilliant final drive (9-of-10, 77 yards) that ended with a 7-yard touchdown pass to Mario Manningham. They couldn't run the ball (58 total yards) and they were having some familiar tackling problems on defense — inexcusable on a day when they finally got most of their injured players back.

Left: Wide receiver Victor Cruz catches, runs and leaps for extra yardage in the second half. *Robert Sabo | Daily News*

Above: Victor Cruz celebrates what turns out to be the game-winning touchdown with his Giants teammates.
Robert Sabo | Daily News

"We weren't as sharp as we thought we were going to be," said Tom Coughlin. "As I told the team, 'That was the bad half. Let's put that behind us and do something about it.'"

They finally started to do that after giving up a field goal to the Dolphins on the opening drive of the second half.

Trailing 17-10, they rallied with 10 fourth-quarter points, including the game-winning pass to Cruz, who broke a tackle by former Giants cornerback Will Allen at the 10.

Then, after Manning gave the Giants a three-point lead, the defense finally took over.

After being unable to contain the slippery Moore for most of the game, they overwhelmed him down the stretch, sacking him four times and picking him off once over his final eight plays.

"We cranked it up because we had to," Coughlin said. "We needed to be in a position where we were putting pressure on the quarterback."

"It was just desire," added linebacker Mathias Kiwanuka. "If we were going to come out victorious we had to do it. We had to do it on defense because we had messed it up in the beginning of the game."

That would've been costly if Manning hadn't "lit it up," as Cruz said, leading the Giants to 402 yards basically on his own. Perhaps more importantly, despite throwing on 68% of the Giants plays (before his three kneel-downs at the end), Manning had no turnovers and no obvious mistakes.

Now the real trick for him is he has to keep playing that way if the Giants want to avoid their traditional second-half collapse, because this nail-biter was the last break on their schedule. Starting on Sunday at New England, the Giants have one of their toughest stretches in years, including games at San Francisco and New Orleans, and a home against the Green Bay Packers, the defending Super Bowl champs.

Asked about that gauntlet yesterday, Coughlin said, "Can we enjoy this one first?"

Thanks to his quarterback, he probably can.

"When there are opportunities to win games, you have to take them," Manning said. "I think we're doing a good job of finding ways to win." ▪

Score by Quarters	1	2	3	4	Final
Miami	7	7	3	0	17
Giants	3	7	0	10	20

OUT OF THE BLUE.

Above: Defensive end Justin Tuck sacks Miami Dolphins quarterback Matt Moore in the second half. *Robert Sabo | Daily News*

SCORING SUMMARY

FIRST QUARTER
DOLPHINS – Slaton 1 run
    (Carpenter kick), 4:10.
GIANTS – FG Tynes 25, :17.

SECOND QUARTER
DOLPHINS – Mat.Moore 1 run
    (Carpenter kick), 9:37.
GIANTS – Manningham 7 pass from Manning
    (Tynes kick), :08.

THIRD QUARTER
DOLPHINS – FG Carpenter 40, 12:17.

FOURTH QUARTER
GIANTS – FG Tynes 29, 10:37.
GIANTS – Cruz 25 pass from Manning
    (Tynes kick), 5:58.

SCORING SUMMARY

	MIA	GIANTS
First downs	18	21
Total Net Yards	246	402
Rushes-yards	26-145	23-58
Passing	101	344
Punt Returns	2-9	4-28
Kickoff Returns	4-99	3-78
Interceptions Ret.	0-0	1-24
Comp-Att-Int	13-22-1	31-45-0
Sacked-Yards Lost	5-37	1-5
Punts	5-49.4	4-46.8
Fumbles-Lost	0-0	1-0
Penalties-Yards	4-30	7-46
Time of Possession	27:34	32:26

Attendance — 79,302

INDIVIDUAL STATISTICS

RUSHING
Miami — Bush 15-103, Mat.Moore 5-31,
    Slaton 5-7, Hilliard 1-4.
Giants — Bradshaw 13-50, Jacobs 4-10,
    Ware 2-1, Manning 4-(minus 3).

PASSING
Miami — Mat.Moore 13-22-1-138.
Giants — Manning 31-45-0-349.

RECEIVING
Miami — Marshall 4-55, Bush 4-17,
    Bess 3-43, Clay 1-16, Hilliard 1-7.
Giants — Cruz 7-99, Nicks 6-67,
    Manningham 6-63, Bradshaw 5-38,
    Ballard 4-55, Pascoe 1-22, Ware 1-5,
    Jacobs 1-0.

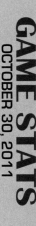

GAME STATS
OCTOBER 30, 2011

PERRY FEWELL

BY RALPH VACCHIANO

The first time the Giants were introduced to Perry Fewell in the spring of 2010, his words were loud and not suitable for children. His voice echoed across the practice field during nearly every play, good or bad.

He brought energy to a unit that had lost it the year before. He restored the players' passion and excitement with every word that came shooting out of his mouth. He came at them like a ball of fire, and in many ways he's never stopped. "He's pretty even-keeled," said linebacker Mathias Kiwanuka. "That's just the keel he's on. He's going to bring his energy and his enthusiasm, but he's not going to go overboard on a mistake or overboard with praise. He's going to tell you what you did wrong or what you did right. That's what we need around here."

Fewell, 49, in his second season as the Giants' defensive coordinator, has always been what the Giants needed, since the moment he walked through the door after Tom Coughlin hired him to replace the unpopular Bill Sheridan in January of 2010. His passion was immediately infectious. His energy was welcomed. He instantly commanded respect.

And don't underestimate that last part when trying to figure out why the Giants' defense has suddenly turned from the battered, beleaguered unit it had been for most of the season into the force of nature that had the Atlanta Falcons — in the words of one Giants defender — "playing scared" in the playoffs.

In the locker room after that 24-2 win over Atlanta, almost every defender gave the credit to Fewell. "He had us prepared to the fullest for everything they presented to us," said safety Antrel Rolle. "I don't think we could've been any more prepared than we were today. Added defensive end Osi Umenyiora: "He called the best game I think I've ever seen called."

Six weeks earlier it didn't seem as if Fewell was feeling that kind of love from anyone. His defense that was ranked seventh in 2010, was sitting near the bottom of the rankings. Then, in an ugly loss in New Orleans, the Giants were barely a speed bump for the Saints' high-powered offense, giving up 49 points and 577 yards. After the loss to the Saints, Fewell erupted — both privately and publicly. Players were beginning to hint they had ques-

Above: Defensive Coordinator Perry Fewell addresses the media after practice.
Corey Sipkin | Daily News

tions about his "scheme" — not an outright mutiny, considering they also voiced their support for their coordinator, but certainly a sign that some things were going wrong. Fewell, backed into a corner, was admittedly upset, and he fought back with a few choice words of his own.

He said his players needed a "kick in the ass to get that motor going." He called their performance "disheartening," said they "were outplayed, outhustled" and essentially accused them of quitting late in the game.

And his players took it, because they knew he was right. "It was a tough situation, and I don't think he showed anything out of his character," Kiwanuka said. "Anybody would've been upset with that kind performance, especially knowing the talent we have around here. There are times he needs to be upset. There are times he needs to be joyful or happy. He's an honest person."

Not every defensive coordinator has been able to get away with that in the Coughlin era. By the time Tim Lewis' three-year reign was over after the 2006 season, players were tired of what they perceived as his constant yelling. Some players — most notably cornerback Corey Webster — were so beaten down they were relieved when he was

Above: Perry Fewell celebrates an interception with defensive back Kenny Phillips. *Ron Antonelli | Daily News*

Below: Fewell has the attention of his defense as he goes over schemes during practice. *Corey Sipkin | Daily News*

finally gone.

And there was Sheridan, the coach with the passionless exterior who bridged the one-year gap (in 2009) from the extremely popular Steve Spagnuolo to Fewell. When Sheridan challenged and criticized his players, they didn't take it well at all.

So how did Fewell get away with it? Again, it all came back to respect. "He's a good man, first and foremost, you understand?" said Umenyiora. "He never really just fell apart or started pointing fingers. He never did that. He always believed that at some point we were going to pull together. He always said that to the defense. Even when we were getting beat up, he was like 'We're a good defense.'

"When you have a defensive coordinator who believes in you like that and believes in himself like that, eventually things will come around. Thankfully that's what happened."

Fewell made believers of his players almost from the moment he took over. In 2010 it worked, he immediately restored their fire and pride, and the results were obvious. The Giants' defense ranked seventh in the league (311.8 yards per game, was fifth in the league with 46 sacks and had 16 interceptions, too.

This year, as the roster crumbled around him, Fewell sold the players on his brilliance as a coach who could adjust. In training camp he lost linebacker Jonathan Goff (torn ACL), cornerback Terrell Thomas (torn ACL) and countless backups. He was forced to go long periods without Umenyiora and a healthy Justin Tuck. So he moved players around, convinced players such as Rolle to play out of position, all for the good of the team. For most of the season the results weren't pretty. But he convinced them to stay the course.

Just as fans began crying for the return of Spagnuolo, the architect of the Super Bowl XLII defense who was recently fired as head coach of the Rams, Fewell got just enough pieces back to prove that he hadn't lost his aggressive touch. "At this point in the season we're healthy enough that we can do most of the things, if not all of the things that he wanted to do," Kiwanuka said. "When he has his full arsenal, we're very confident in what he can draw up."

Coughlin never lost faith in his former defensive backs coach from his days in Jacksonville (1998-2002). "Perry is a terrific coordinator," GM Jerry Reese said. "He's taken a lot of heat and that's what you do in this town — you take heat. It's what this town is all about and you have to relish the heat. And I think we do."

"He didn't really care what you people say," Tuck said. "It would be easy for him to read the newspaper and see 'This person got fired and he might be up for the coaching job.' He didn't allow any of that to distract him. He continued to press forward and continued to try to do his job at the highest level.

"We've all benefitted from that."∎

OUT OF THE BLUE.

GAME EIGHT
GIANTS 24 | PATRIOTS 20

THERE WASN'T A SILVER TROPHY, BUT THE WIN HAD A FAMILIAR RING TO IT

BY RALPH VACCHIANO

There was no confetti floating in the air when it was over, and nobody handed the Giants a silver trophy. Their win over the New England Patriots Sunday sure did have a familiar ring to it, though.

It included not one, but two remarkable fourth-quarter comebacks by Eli Manning. There was a dazzling catch over the middle on the final drive by tight end Jake Ballard, who just happens to wear David Tyree's old No. 85. The game-winning touchdown pass went to the left corner of the end zone, just like it did four years ago in Glendale, Ariz.

And when they were done shocking the world in a game that played out eerily similar to their big upset in Super Bowl XLII, the Giants (6-2) even celebrated their 24-20

Left: Tight end Jake Ballard scores the winning touchdown as the Giants beat New England 24-20. *Andrew Theodorakis | Daily News*

win over the Patriots like champions, with embattled running back Brandon Jacobs lifting Tom Coughlin onto his shoulders in the locker room for a little postgame ride.

"It was unbelievable," said defensive end Osi Umenyiora. "It was a big win for us. Nobody gave us a chance. Half our offense wasn't here and we still came up here and beat a great football team."

Added Ballard, who made his leaping, 28-yard third-down catch without the aid of his helmet: "I think it shows a lot of people we are for real."

It should, because the Giants not only snapped the Patriots' 20-game regular-season home winning streak, they did it without their best receiver (Hakeem Nicks), starting running back (Ahmad Bradshaw) and starting center (David Baas). Most of the credit for that goes to Manning (20-for-39, 250 yards, two touchdowns, one interception), who shook off a slow start and one critical mistake in the third quarter to lead the Giants back from the brink of defeat twice.

It was the type of performance, as so many of his teammates said after the game, that "elite" quarterbacks give. In fact, to those who still doubt Manning belongs in a class with Brady, defensive end Justin Tuck said, "You go track those fans down and ask them what they think of him now. I think he had the last laugh in this one."

Added Jacobs: "To me he's better than 12 (Brady). 12 couldn't get it done today. 10 got it done."

At first, Manning almost didn't. Sitting at the New England 2-yard line late in the third quarter with a chance to take a two-touchdown lead, Manning was picked off in the

Above: Brandon Jacobs shakes things up in the end zone after scoring the first touchdown of the game. *Corey Sipkin* | *Daily News*

end zone by cornerback Kyle Arrington. That opened the door for Brady (28-for-49, 342 yards, two touchdowns, two interceptions) to shake off his struggles from a surprisingly scoreless first half and drive for a 5-yard touchdown pass to tight end Aaron Hernandez early in the fourth that tied the game 10-10.

The Patriots (5-3) then took a 13-10 lead on a 45-yard Stephen Gostkowski field goal with 7:08 remaining, setting the stage for Manning comeback No. 1. With the help of a huge pass interference penalty on Arrington, Manning led the Giants to a 10-yard touchdown pass to Mario Manningham - also to the left corner of the end zone - giving the Giants a 17-13 lead.

Unlike the Super Bowl, though, when he threw the winning touchdown pass with 35 seconds left, this time he left Brady plenty of time. And the Patriots' quarterback put on his own magic show, with a fourth-down, 14-yard touchdown pass to tight end Rob Gronkowski with just 1:36 left in the game.

The Giants weren't worried.

SCORE BY QUARTERS	1	2	3	4	FINAL
Giants	0	0	10	14	24
New England	0	0	3	17	20

OUT OF THE BLUE:

Above: The Giants' defense swarms around a Patriots' running back to bring him down.
Andrew Theodorakis | *Daily News*

"Fortunately enough," Manning said, "they scored real quick and left us with enough time to get a good drive."

"No matter what happened today we weren't going to fold," added safety Antrel Rolle. "No matter what adversity we were going to go through, no matter how hard they were pushing, we were going to make sure we were going to stand up against that wall and make sure we respond."

They did, behind Manning. And the moment they knew they were going to win came on a third-and-10 from the Patriots' 39 when he found Ballard over the middle to make a leaping, Tyree-like catch.

"I knew we were going to win the game (then)," said Jacobs, who had 100 total yards rushing and receiving. "It kind of brought me back to the Super Bowl. When we make a catch like that in the middle of the field, and go down and score, we got it."

Five plays later, with the help of another pass interference penalty, this time on safety Sergio Brown, the Giants had it. Manning went back to the Burress corner again, this time for Ballard with 15 seconds remaining.

Then came the party, with Coughlin in the air "thinking they were going to drop me on my head," he said.

"This is a huge win," Tuck said. "This team was unbeatable here."

"We did something that hasn't been done in a long time," Rolle added. "We all came together at the right time and we proved a point." ∎

SCORING SUMMARY

THIRD QUARTER
GIANTS – FG Tynes 22, 10:09.
GIANTS – Jacobs 10 run (Tynes kick), 9:10.
PATRIOTS – FG Gostkowski 32, 5:29.

FOURTH QUARTER
PATRIOTS – Hernandez 5 pass from Brady
  (Gostkowski kick), 14:28.
PATRIOTS – FG Gostkowski 45, 7:08.
GIANTS – Manningham 10 pass from Manning
  (Tynes kick), 3:03.
PATRIOTS – R.Gronkowski 14 pass from Brady
  (Gostkowski kick), 1:36.
GIANTS – Ballard 1 pass from Manning
  (Tynes kick), :15.

SCORING SUMMARY

	GIANTS	NE
First downs	23	23
Total Net Yards	361	438
Rushes-yards	29-111	24-106
Passing	250	332
Punt Returns	1-0	5-17
Kickoff Returns	4-61	5-97
Interceptions Ret.	2-9	1-0
Comp-Att-Int	20-39-1	28-49-2
Sacked-Yards Lost	0-0	2-10
Punts	8-43.1	5-45.0
Fumbles-Lost	2-1	2-2
Penalties-Yards	6-50	7-81
Time of Possession	30:17	29:43

Attendance — 68,756

INDIVIDUAL STATISTICS

RUSHING
Giants — Jacobs 18-72, Ware 7-23,
  Manning 3-11, Scott 1-5.
New England — Green-Ellis 12-52,
  Woodhead 7-26, Welker 1-13, Ridley 3-10,
  Brady 1-5.

PASSING
Giants — Manning 20-39-1-250.
New England — Brady 28-49-2-342.

RECEIVING
Giants — Cruz 6-91, Ballard 4-67, Jacobs 4-28,
  Manningham 3-33, Barden 2-24, Pascoe 1-7.
New England — Welker 9-136,
  R.Gronkowski 8-101, Hernandez 4-35,
  Woodhead 3-34, Branch 2-21,
  Green-Ellis 1-11, Ridley 1-2, Edelman 0-2.

MISSED FIELD GOALS
New England — Gostkowski 27 (WL).

GAME STATS
NOVEMBER 6, 2011

OUT OF THE BLUE.

GAME NINE
49ERS 27 | GIANTS 20

YOU CAN ONLY PLAY WITH FIRE SO MANY TIMES WITHOUT GETTING BURNED, TODAY THEY GOT BURNED

BY RALPH VACCHIANO

The Giants have spent the first half of their season trying to defy logic, to test the theory that you can only play with fire so many times and survive. They were good at it. They were comfortable. They weren't afraid of being burned.

So when they finally were burned on Sunday, when they found a deficit too big to overcome, something that even Eli Manning's magic couldn't pull them out of, maybe they had it coming. Maybe it shouldn't have been so shocking.

Maybe the Giants suffering a frustrating defeat like their 27-20 loss to the 49ers on Sunday was only a matter of time.

"I'm not shocked," said Giants defensive end Osi Umenyiora. "We shouldn't keep letting it get like that."

No they shouldn't, but they do and they have all season. Until Sunday, it had been one of the most endearing parts of their story. The Giants (6-3) have lived on the edge, and Eli Manning has been Captain Comeback, leading the charge back from fourth-quarter deficits four times this season, giving rise to an impressive first half of the season and his fringe candidacy for league MVP.

But this time, when the Giants fell behind in the fourth quarter for, incredibly, the seventh time in nine games, the miracle comeback fell short.

First, with 2:50 remaining, he led Mario Manningham just a bit too far on what would've been a 42-yard touchdown. Then, in the closing seconds, after two big fourth-down completions, he had his third fourth-down pass tipped

Above: Mario Manningham has six catches on the day, but can't quite haul this pass in. *Marcio Jose Sanchez | AP Photo*

Left: Running back DJ Ware fights for yardage against a tough San Francisco defense. *Tom DiPace | AP Photo*

Above: Eli Manning can't escape the grasp of 49ers linebacker Patrick Willis as Big Blue has a rough afternoon in San Fran. *Marcio Jose Sanchez | AP Photo*

SCORE BY QUARTERS	1	2	3	4	FINAL
Giants	**3**	**3**	**7**	**7**	**20**
San Francisco	**3**	**6**	**3**	**15**	**27**

OUT OF THE BLUE.

at the line of scrimmage before it could reach a possibly open Victor Cruz.

Until the moment 49ers defensive tackle Justin Smith batted that pass, the Giants were absolutely convinced they were going to win — again. That was true even after a 17-yard run by rookie Kendall Hunter had put the 49ers up by two touchdowns with 12:21 remaining. Never mind that Manning was starting to struggle after his 10-for-10 start. And never mind that the 49ers had rediscovered their ground attack after losing Frank Gore to a knee injury.

The Giants, in Tom Coughlin's words, felt like they were "in perfect control."

"Yeah, I'm very disappointed," Coughlin said. "We've done very, very well in those situations and I expected to do well again. It didn't happen, and you can call it percentages or whatever you want, but we're prepared to excel in that area. We've done just that."

So far this season the Giants have had fourth-quarter, come-from-behind victories over the Eagles, Cardinals, Dolphins and most recently — and dramatically — the Patriots. They have also come back from a fourth-quarter tie with the Bills thanks mostly to Manning, who has been one of the best fourth-quarter quarterbacks in the NFL.

The truth, though, is that it's not an easy formula to sustain and the fact that the Giants have trailed or been tied in the fourth quarter of all but one of their games this season is a very dangerous sign. They may have one of the best records in the NFC and still be sitting in first in their division, but they're also an injury-riddled team getting by with some overachieving play by replacement players, led by a quarterback in the midst of a remarkable year.

The problem is that at some point the clock strikes midnight and Cinderella's coach turns back into a pumpkin. It happens in almost every fairy tale. The only question, usually, is when.

Whether this Giants loss is a sign that it's happening now, or that they're on the brink of yet another second-half collapse, will become clearer in the coming weeks, especially with the Eagles, Saints and Packers coming up next on the Giants' treacherous schedule. But one thing should be certain: If they continue to play from the edge of their seats and rely on the tips of their fingers, they're only setting themselves up to get burned again.

"We had confidence until the very end and next week we'll still have confidence if we're put in that situation again," said guard Chris Snee. "It's not something we're going to lose just because we came up a little short. We're confident that when the game is on the line we're going to get it done. More often than not we do."

But not always, and that's the worry. The Giants can only hope they saved more magic for the second half.

"We felt confident," Manning said. "We were right there. Very close."

Close, as they learned on Sunday, isn't always good enough. ∎

SCORING SUMMARY

FIRST QUARTER
GIANTS – FG Tynes 23, 6:27.
49ERS – FG Akers 36, :25.

SECOND QUARTER
GIANTS – FG Tynes 25, 9:05.
49ERS – FG Akers 52, 5:00.
49ERS – FG Akers 39, 1:49.

THIRD QUARTER
49ERS – FG Akers 28, 11:14.
GIANTS – Manningham 13 pass from Manning (Tynes kick), 2:25.

FOURTH QUARTER
49ERS – V.Davis 31 pass from Ale.Smith (Crabtree pass from Ale.Smith), 13:22.
49ERS – Hunter 17 run (Akers kick), 12:21.
GIANTS – Nicks 32 pass from Manning (Tynes kick), 8:37.

SCORING SUMMARY

	GIANTS	SF
First downs	21	16
Total Net Yards	395	305
Rushes-yards	29-93	20-77
Passing	302	228
Punt Returns	3-12	0-0
Kickoff Returns	2-53	2-55
Interceptions Ret.	1-6	2-17
Comp-Att-Int	26-40-2	19-30-1
Sacked-Yards Lost	1-9	2-14
Punts	2-38.5	3-54.7
Fumbles-Lost	0-0	0-0
Penalties-Yards	6-45	5-35
Time of Possession	34:37	25:23

Attendance — 69,732

INDIVIDUAL STATISTICS

RUSHING
Giants — Jacobs 18-55, Ware 9-34, Manning 2-4.
San Francisco — Hunter 6-40, Ale.Smith 6-27, Dixon 2-10, Gore 6-0.

PASSING
Giants — Manning 26-40-2-311.
San Francisco — Ale.Smith 19-30-1-242.

RECEIVING
Giants — Cruz 6-84, Manningham 6-77, Ware 5-34, Ballard 3-35, Nicks 2-41, Pascoe 2-23, Jacobs 2-17.
San Francisco — Walker 6-69, Edwards 3-47, V.Davis 3-40, Ginn Jr. 3-39, Crabtree 1-21, K.Williams 1-14, Gore 1-8, Hunter 1-4.

OUT OF THE BLUE.

EAGLES 17 | GIANTS 10

THEIR PATHETIC PERFORMANCE MAKES ONE THING VERY CLEAR TO EVERYONE

BY RALPH VACCHIANO

The Giants knew there was no sense in trying to deny it, and they knew they had nowhere to run and hide. Their pathetic performance made one thing clear to anyone who saw it:

Their annual second-half collapse has begun.

Maybe they can stop the slide in the coming weeks, but they looked helpless on Sunday night against the Philadelphia Eagles. Given a chance to bury their bitter rivals and cling to their lead in the NFC East, the Giants looked more like pretenders than contenders as they fell meekly at the Meadowlands to the once-dead Dream Team, 17-10.

And though this loss wasn't as dramatic as their collapse against the Eagles at the Meadowlands last season, it was equally crushing. The Eagles broke a fourth-quarter tie with a slow, torturous, 18-play, 80-yard, 8:51 march that ended with an 8-yard touchdown pass from backup quarterback Vince Young to Riley Cooper with 2:45 remaining.

The Giants' last chance for a miracle ended at the Eagles' 21 with 1:17 left when the Giants' struggling offensive line gave up one last sack to defensive end Jason Babin, who forced an Eli Manning fumble that Philadelphia recovered.

And with that, the Giants (6-4) dropped into a first-place tie with the Dallas Cowboys, with the dangerous Eagles (4-6) lurking just two games behind.

"That's as big a disappointment as we've had around here in a long time," said Tom Coughlin. "I didn't like the way we played. It was a very poor performance."

For most of the game, it was mostly the offense that was poor. Behind an offensive line that Coughlin said "got physically manhandled," Manning completed 18 of 35 passes for 264 yards, but couldn't find the end zone until he hit Victor Cruz (six catches, 128 yards) with a 24-yard touchdown pass that tied the game in the fourth quarter.

It didn't help that his receivers dropped at least five passes, including three by usually reliable tight end Jake Ballard. The Giants' running game was "pathetic" as well, in Coughlin's words,

Left: Cornerback Aaron Ross intercepts a pass in the second half.
Ron Antonelli | *Daily News*

with just 29 yards on 17 carries. Brandon Jacobs, who carried 12 times for just 21 yards, called the performance "the worst I've ever experienced in my seven years of playing here."

"(We) just couldn't get anything going," Manning said. "We just never got in a rhythm at all."

The Giants were in the game because the defense picked off three of the erratic Young's passes and in the first half only surrendered a 14-yard touchdown pass from Young (23-of-36, 258 yards) to former Giants receiver Steve Smith that was set up by a DeSean Jackson 51-yard punt return. When Manning found Cruz in the end zone with 11:36 remaining, the Giants seemed poised for their fifth fourth-quarter comeback of the year.

Instead, the Eagles (4-6) put together a drive that lasted 34 seconds longer than the 8:17 they needed to score four touchdowns at the end of their 38-31 win at the Meadowlands last December. They converted all six of their third downs on the drive against the Giants' Michael Boley-less defense.

Above: Hakeem Nicks hauls in one of just three catches he has against the Eagles. *Robert Sabo | Daily News*

"Yeah, that hurts," said linebacker Mathias Kiwanuka. "That's not acceptable."

None of it was acceptable, which is why Coughlin was so livid after the game. He said he was sure that after their narrow, 27-20 loss in San Francisco his team would respond to an opportunity to put the Eagles away. He told them they were dangerous, even with Michael Vick injured.

He thought his players had listened all week long.

"My question to them was 'Why?' " Coughlin said. "What did it take to understand what the Eagles were going to be like coming in here? You don't have to be a rocket scientist to know the team is 3-6, backs to the wall, they're going to play their butts off.

"I'm really disappointed. Coming off San Francisco the talk was, by the players, 'We'll

fight. We'll play hard. We'll do all those things.' I didn't see that."

He'll need to see that fight now, because the Giants have set themselves up for a battle - and not just because they've begun to ruin their 6-2 start with an 0-2 beginning to the second half. Next up is a dangerous trip to New Orleans to play the Saints (7-3) next Monday night, followed by a home game one week later against the defending Super Bowl-champion Green Bay Packers (10-0).

Then they play the first of two games against the Cowboys (6-4), who could be in charge of the NFC East by then.

"Every game is important now," Manning said. "Every game is big and we have to have a little rally."

"It's very disappointing," Kiwanuka added. "The only bright side I can think of is we still have a lot of games to play." ∎

SCORE BY QUARTERS	1	2	3	4	FINAL
Philadelphia	0	10	0	7	17
Giants	0	3	0	7	10

OUT OF THE BLUE:

Above: Eli Manning is brought down in the first half, it's one of three Eagles sacks on the day. *Robert Sabo* | *Daily News*

SCORING SUMMARY

SECOND QUARTER
EAGLES – FG Henery 33, 11:31.
EAGLES – Smith 14 pass from Young
 (Henery kick), 1:22.
GIANTS – FG Tynes 48, :00.

FOURTH QUARTER
GIANTS – Cruz 24 pass from Manning
 (Tynes kick), 11:36.
EAGLES – Cooper 8 pass from Young
 (Henery kick), 2:45.

SCORING SUMMARY

	PHI	GIANTS
First downs	17	12
Total Net Yards	391	278
Rushes-yards	33-136	17-29
Passing	255	249
Punt Returns	4-63	0-0
Kickoff Returns	1-26	3-61
Interceptions Ret.	1-14	3-6
Comp-Att-Int	23-36-3	18-35-1
Sacked-Yards Lost	1-3	3-15
Punts	6-43.5	9-51.4
Fumbles-Lost	0-0	1-1
Penalties-Yards	5-30	5-39
Time of Possession	36:18	23:42

Attendance — 79,743

INDIVIDUAL STATISTICS

RUSHING
 Philadelphia — McCoy 23-113, Hall 2-11,
  Brown 1-6, Young 6-5, Lewis 1-1.
 Giants — Jacobs 12-21, Scott 2-11,
  Ware 3-(minus 3).

PASSING
 Philadelphia — Young 23-36-3-258.
 Giants — Manning 18-35-1-264.

RECEIVING
 Philadelphia — D.Jackson 6-88, Celek 6-60,
  Cooper 5-75, McCoy 3-2, Smith 1-14,
  Avant 1-13, Harbor 1-6.
 Giants — Cruz 6-128, Nicks 3-69,
  Jacobs 3-11, Ware 2-17, Ballard 1-13,
  Barden 1-13, Scott 1-9, Manningham 1-4.

GAME STATS
NOVEMBER 20, 2011

ELI MANNING

BY RALPH VACCHIANO

Eli Manning has exceeded almost every expectation in the months since he famously announced to the world on ESPN Radio that he was an elite, Top 5 quarterback.

He shattered his career best in several statistical categories and some of the Giants' single-season passing records, too. While playing for a banged-up, under-manned team, he dragged the Giants to a 6-2 start, and at times, almost single-handedly kept them in the playoff race.

He obviously knew he could do it all along and his teammates say they knew it, too.

"I don't think I'm surprised by anything he's done," defensive end Justin Tuck said. "I'm impressed, obviously, but surprised? No. I think this is probably his best year as a pro and with good reason. He was setting up all those offseason workouts with running backs and wide receivers during the lockout. And he worked his butt off to become the quarterback he's become.

"I give (him) a lot of credit considering the shadows that he's had to play under being Archie's son and Peyton's little brother and playing in a city like New York where it just seems sometimes you can never do enough," Tuck continued. "So I'm very proud to call him my teammate and quarterback. It's been awesome to watch him play."

Manning's play this season has gone beyond his numbers, which were spectacular. He shattered the franchise record with 4,933 yards, completed more than 60% of his passes for the fourth straight season and threw for 29 touchdowns while dropping his interceptions from 25 in 2010 to 16. He also led the Giants back from a fourth-quarter deficit to a win five times during the regular season and set an NFL record with 15 touchdown passes in the fourth quarter.

Look what he has done down the stretch in four straight elimination games (the regular-season finale plus three more in the playoffs): he completed 64.1% of his passes (100 of 156) for 1,269 yards, 11 touchdowns and just one interception. In those four wins, that's a passer rating of 100.2.

Not that Antrel Rolle needed to be convinced,

Above: Eli Manning reacts to throwing a fourth-quarter touchdown against the 49ers in the NFC Championship game.
Andrew Theodorakis | Daily News

but the veteran safety seemed particularly taken aback by Manning's performance in the NFC Championship Game. The quarterback completed 32 of 58 passes for 316 yards and two touchdowns on a rainy, windy night at Candlestick Park — and he did it while taking six sacks and absorbing 12 sometimes brutal hits.

"He's a leader, man," Rolle said. "Him going out there and doing what he did, I think that definite-

OUT OF THE BLUE.

Above: Like his brother Peyton, Eli Manning is strong at directing traffic at the line of scrimmage. *Ron Antonelli | Daily News*

ly exemplifies what kind of guy he is and what kind of leadership (he has). A lot of people question — just because of the facial expressions that he may make — how much fight does he have? How tough is he?

"Let's put it this way," Rolle continued. "If he can withstand what he did going up against the 49ers and their front seven, you can't question his toughness."

There's not much that can be questioned about Manning anymore. Now 31 and in his eighth NFL season, he has a chance to win a second Super Bowl ring - something his Hall of Fame-bound brother Peyton doesn't have. Eli proved he was right when he said back in August, "I'm not a 25-interception quarterback." While Tom Brady was better statistically (65.6 completion rate, 5,235 yards, 39 touchdowns, 12 interceptions), Manning undoubtedly stepped up to his level this season.

The Patriots always believe they have a chance to win because they have Brady. Now the Giants, because of Manning, believe that, too.

"Eli and Tom are two of the more elite quarterbacks in this league, and when you have people like that leading the charge, you are never out of a football game," Tuck said. "If you ask the Patriots that same question, I am sure they will say the same thing. In the fourth quarter and (if) it is close, they feel like they are going to bring it out

because they have a quarterback like Tom, and we feel the same way."

That was Manning's point back in August, when he was asked if he believed he was a "Top 10, Top 5" quarterback and he responded, "Yeah, I think I am." Then he was asked if he was on Brady's level, and he added, "Yeah, I consider myself in that class. And Tom Brady is a great quarterback."

Manning said on Tuesday, "I don't have any regrets" about the statement that set the tone for his breakout season, adding, "Obviously it's been made into a big deal, but I can't always control that."

It wasn't just a big deal to his critics and his fans, though. It was a big deal to some of his teammates, too - especially when he went out and spent the season backing his big words up.

"It means a lot," Rolle said. "It lets me know what kind of guy we have leading this team. Eli is the leader of this team, without a doubt, and I wouldn't be standing up here right now if it wasn't for him. He is an elite quarterback. I don't think that needs any further discussion. I think he's definitely proven himself. . . . When it's all said and done you have to know yourself. You just have to believe within yourself.

"And that's what he does."■

OUT OF THE BLUE.

GAME ELEVEN
SAINTS 49 | GIANTS 24

THINGS ARE STARTING TO GET A LITTLE HOTTER FOR ELI & COUGHLIN

BY RALPH VACCHIANO

The pressure will now be turned up on Eli Manning to continue to prove he's "elite." The heat will get turned up soon on Tom Coughlin to once again find a way to save his job.

But if this Giants' collapse, now seemingly in full swing, becomes the "historical" disaster that Justin Tuck warned it could, don't blame the quarterback and don't blame the coach. This franchise used to be known for a strong defense and a devastating pass rush.

Now both have all but disappeared.

They were absolutely shredded Monday night by the New Orleans Saints in a 49-24 rout that was nearly "historical" and could've been much worse.

Drew Brees, on his way to 363 yards, had so much time in the pocket he could've set up a lawn chair and thrown passes with a drink in his hands. He was never short of open receivers exploiting the gaps in the gap-filled Giants' secondary.

By halftime, Brees had already thrown for 265 yards and three touchdowns. The Saints had 354 yards of offense by then, on their way to what Antrel Rolle said was an "unacceptable" total of 577.

It wasn't just unacceptable, it was one of the worst defensive performances in franchise history — the second-most yards they've ever allowed in a game, the most being the 682 piled up by the Bears on Nov. 14, 1943, in a 56-7 romp.

Left: Victor Cruz tries to find daylight against the Saints as DJ Ware throws a block for him. *Jim Mahoney | AP Photo*

Worse, the Giants didn't seem to have any idea as to how or why it happened, which is another part of this increasingly disturbing defensive trend.

"We've got to look at the film and take a serious look at how they were able to basically do whatever they wanted," said defensive end Mathias Kiwanuka. "We didn't play fast enough. We didn't play hard enough."

"Obviously we had a tough time stopping them," added Coughlin. "They're good. They're talented. They did a good job of spreading the ball out. Their quarterback does a good job of getting the ball out of his hands fast.

"Wejust weren't able to cover them." They haven't been able to consistently cover anyone all

Above: Eli Manning throws for two touchdowns, but it is nowhere near enough against the high-powered Saints. *Bill Haber | AP Photo*

SCORE BY QUARTERS	1	2	3	4	FINAL
Giants	0	3	7	14	24
New Orleans	0	21	14	14	49

OUT OF THE BLUE.

season, so that wasn't much of a surprise. The surprise has been the strange and sudden disappearance of a pass rush that was once among the most feared in the league. They entered the weekend with an NFL-leading 31 sacks and were stuck on that number after getting zero against Brees. They were credited with six quarterback hits, but even that seemed like a stretch considering the defense barely bothered the Saints quarterback at all.

"We were close a couple of times, but we weren't effective enough in disrupting what they wanted to do," said defensive tackle Chris Canty. "They kind of did what they wanted to do. We didn't put enough consistent   pressure to make them uncomfortable."

That wouldn't be so alarming if it wasn't a trend. Since their five-sack performance in a win over the Miami Dolphins on Oct. 30, they've had just five sacks and 14 quarterback hits in the last four games. Perry Fewell, the Giants' defensive coordinator, was asked last week where his pass rush has gone, and he said, "I can't put my finger on" the answer.

He better do it soon, though, because if Brees can slice through his defense like he did on Monday night, what is Aaron Rodgers going do when the undefeated Green Bay Packers come to the Meadowlands on Sunday afternoon? The Packers are better and more explosive. Rodgers is more accurate and has more weapons.

If Rodgers gets the kind of time to sit back in the pocket that Brees had on Monday night, the reeling Giants (6-5) will have absolutely no chance to stop their three-game losing streak.

And then they'll have to travel to Dallas to face Tony Romo, another elusive quarterback, with their season on the line.

There are plenty of reasons for this unfathomable defensive meltdown.

Tuck, thanks to injuries, is a shell of his old self and only has two sacks.

Osi Umenyiora has slowed down considerably and now has an ankle injury that ended his game in the first quarter on Monday night. Jason Pierre-Paul (two sacks in the last four games) looks, as Fewell seemed to fear a few weeks ago, as if he's overworked and slowing down.

The reasons almost don't matter, though, because time is running out on the Giants' once-promising season. Manning can't do it alone, and it's clear he won't get any help from the Giants' "pathetic" rushing attack.

The secondary and young linebacking corps will be stretched thin in the next few weeks, too.

That puts the pressure on the men who are supposed to deliver it on defense.

They're the ones with the Giants' season in their hands.■

SCORING SUMMARY

SECOND QUARTER
SAINTS – Moore 4 pass from Brees [Kasay kick], 14:52.
GIANTS – FG Tynes 42, 9:30.
SAINTS – Graham 5 pass from Brees [Kasay kick], 2:21.
SAINTS – Moore 10 pass from Brees [Kasay kick], :35.

THIRD QUARTER
GIANTS – Jacobs 8 run [Tynes kick], 10:43.
SAINTS – Brees 8 run [Kasay kick], 5:48.
SAINTS – Graham 29 pass from Brees [Kasay kick], 4:13.

FOURTH QUARTER
GIANTS – Cruz 72 pass from Manning [Tynes kick], 14:50.
SAINTS – P.Thomas 12 run [Kasay kick], 10:41.
GIANTS – Cruz 4 pass from Manning [Tynes kick], 5:12.
SAINTS – Ingram 35 run [Kasay kick], 1:02.

SCORING SUMMARY

	GIANTS	NO
First downs	29	31
Total Net Yards	465	577
Rushes-yards	22-73	30-205
Passing	392	372
Punt Returns	1-[-1]	0-0
Kickoff Returns	4-115	3-64
Interceptions Ret.	0-0	1-0
Comp-Att-Int	33-47-1	25-39-0
Sacked-Yards Lost	1-14	0-0
Punts	2-38.0	2-42.0
Fumbles-Lost	4-1	0-0
Penalties-Yards	4-32	11-104
Time of Possession	31:28	28:32

Attendance — 73,068

INDIVIDUAL STATISTICS

RUSHING
Giants — Jacobs 13-46, Ware 5-23, Manning 1-4, Scott 2-0, Weatherford 1-0.
New Orleans — Ingram 13-80, P.Thomas 8-63, Sproles 8-54, Brees 1-8.

PASSING
Giants — Manning 33-47-1-406.
New Orleans — Brees 24-38-0-363, Daniel 1-1-0-9.

RECEIVING
Giants — Cruz 9-157, Ware 8-45, Nicks 7-87, Ballard 3-47, Barden 3-38, D.Thomas 1-12, Hynoski 1-10, Pascoe 1-10.
New Orleans — Graham 5-84, Henderson 5-67, Moore 5-54, Colston 3-78, P.Thomas 3-47, Sproles 2-28, Ingram 2-14.

MISSED FIELD GOALS
Giants — Tynes 61 (SH).

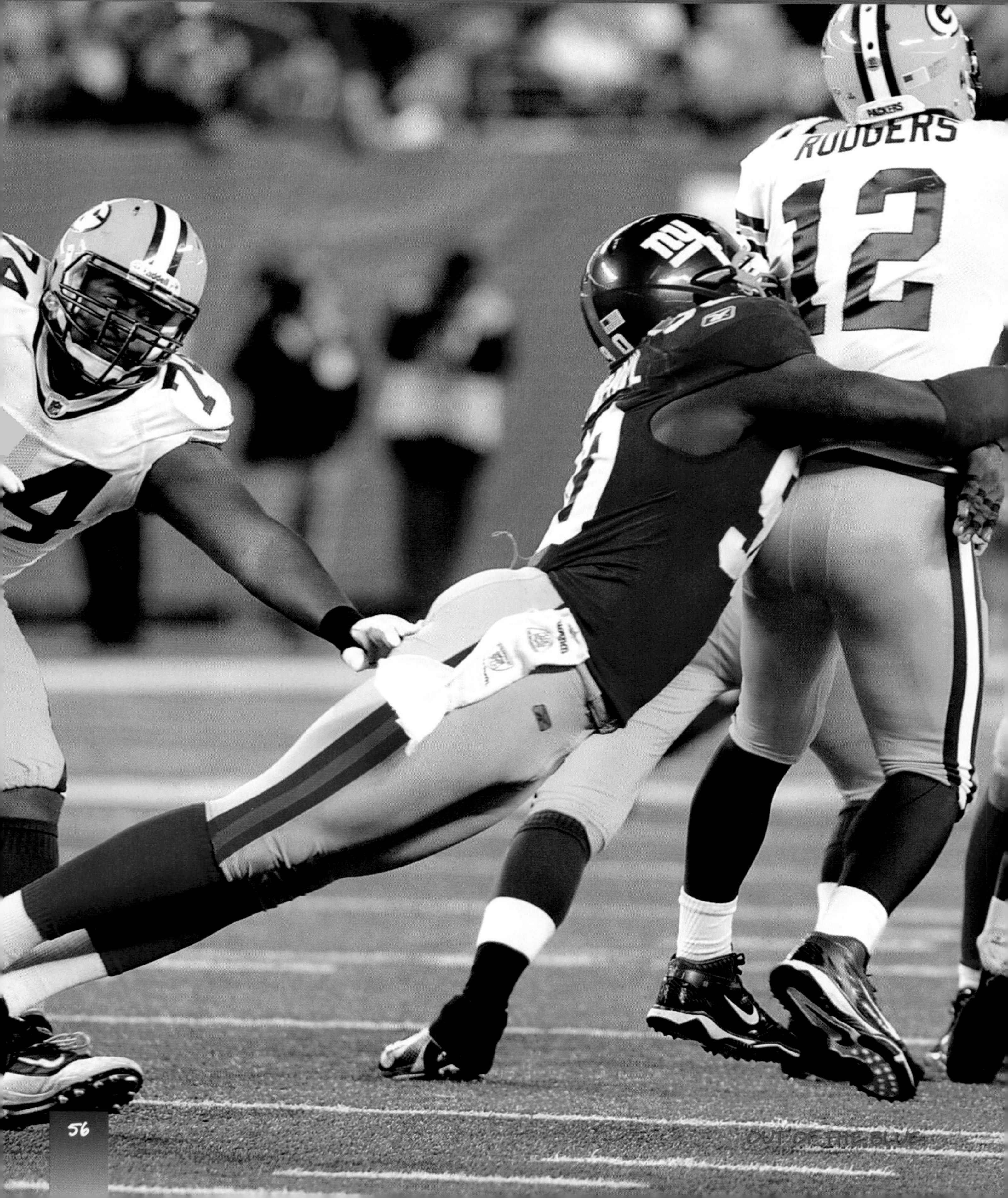
RODGERS
12

GAME TWELVE
PACKERS 38 | GIANTS 35

BIG BLUE IN DESPERATE NEED OF MOMENTUM

BY RALPH VACCHIANO

They know from their own history what a loss such as this one can do. They know that a wave of momentum can be created by pushing an unbeaten team to the brink.

Maybe some day this will seem like an important moral victory for the Giants.

It just didn't feel that way on Sunday night.

"It feels like we lost four in a row," Justin Tuck said after the Giants lost, 38-35, to the defending Super Bowl champion Green Bay Packers at MetLife Stadium. "I'm sick to my stomach. And I hope all my teammates feel the same way."

It appeared that most of them did, despite their impressive effort against a team that has now won 18 straight games dating back to last December. Just six days after getting embarrassed in New Orleans, the Giants didn't let the Packers escape the Meadowlands until Mason Crosby's 31-yard field goal with no time remaining.

It was an impressive rebound, to be sure, for a very undermanned Giants team. But the reality was that after the Giants tied the score with 58 seconds remaining on a 2-yard touchdown pass from Eli Manning to Hakeem Nicks and a two-point conversion run by D.J. Ware, Green Bay quarterback Aaron Rodgers needed only two big pass plays to set up the game-winning field goal.

When the kick was good, the Giants had lost their fourth straight game and turned their once-promising 6-2 start into a disappointing

Left: Defensive end Jason Pierre-Paul grabs hold of Aaron Rodgers, but the Packers QB still throws for four TDs.
Robert Sabo | Daily News

57

.500 record. Thanks to the Arizona Cardinals' overtime win over the Dallas Cowboys, the Giants (6-6) are still very much alive in the NFC East, but they're still one game back as they head into a division showdown in Dallas on Sunday night.

"Obviously you can feel good about your effort, but you didn't win," said defensive end Dave Tollefson. "And that trumps everything."

"Obviously we can build on this momentum," Tuck added. "But we let another one slip out of our fingers. It still hurts."

It hurts for a lot of reasons, including that the Giants wasted yet another terrific effort from Manning, who stood toe-to-toe with Rodgers, the likely NFL MVP, by completing 23 of 40 passes for 347 yards and three touchdowns. That included a tone-setting, 67-yard touchdown pass to little-used tight end Travis Beckum on the third play of the game. Rodgers completed 28 of 46 passes for 369 yards and four touchdowns. Each threw a costly interception that led to a touchdown as well.

And despite losing his starting center two hours before kickoff when David Baas was scratched due to headaches, Manning was even on the verge of leading another fourth-quarter comeback. Trailing 28-24 entering the fourth, he helped the Giants pull within a point on a 50-yard Lawrence Tynes field goal after he just missed connecting with Nicks on what would've been a 32-yard touchdown pass.

The Packers (12-0) reasserted control when Rodgers completed his second touchdown pass to Donald Driver, who barely got his feet inbounds with 3:34 remaining to give Green Bay a 35-27 lead. But Manning came out firing again, quickly moving to set up the Nicks touchdown. And when Ware added the two points on a shotgun draw, the game was tied and the Meadowlands was rocking.

"I thought we were in pretty good shape," Tom Coughlin said. "Fifty-eight seconds left, we should get that thing to overtime."

"We came in prepared to shock the world,"

Tuck said. "I don't think there was any time in the game where we didn't feel like we were going to win the game."

But they didn't because Rodgers quickly hit tight end Jermichael Finley for 24 yards. Then he found Jordy Nelson being covered by the recently signed Will Blackmon, who was filling in for the fatigued Prince Amukamara, and hit him for 29 yards to put the Packers well within range of the game-winning field goal.

An 18-yarder to Greg Jennings only made it easier.

It was a disappointing end, especially for a defense that gave a much better effort after giving up 577 yards to the Saints six days earlier and earning a tounge-lashing from defensive coordinator Perry Fewell. The Giants gave up 449 yards, but generated a consistent pass rush on Rodgers, even with the injured Osi Umenyiora out.

Still, as Coughlin said, "No solace in playing well and losing. We're way past that."

Maybe. Then again, no one has forgotten what happened in 2007 after the Giants lost by the same score, 38-35, to the unbeaten New England Patriots in the regular-season finale. They rode that wave of confidence all the way to an upset of the Patriots in Super Bowl XLII.

Could it happen again? "I would hope that would be the case," Coughlin said. "Those are the kind of emotional things that bind you together."

"When we put our minds to it, anything is possible as a team," safety Antrel Rolle added. "We're going to fight to get in these playoffs. And once we get into the playoffs there's not going to be anything that can stop us."■

SCORE BY QUARTERS	1	2	3	4	FINAL
Green Bay	7	14	7	10	38
Giants	10	7	7	11	35

Above: Wide receiver Hakeem Nicks touchdown catch in the 4th quarter of the Giants 38-35 loss. *Ron Antonelli | Daily News*

SCORING SUMMARY

FIRST QUARTER
GIANTS – Beckum 67 pass from Manning
    (Tynes kick), 13:24.
PACKERS – Finley 12 pass from Rodgers
    (Crosby kick), 5:06.
GIANTS – FG Tynes 38, 2:00.

SECOND QUARTER
PACKERS – Matthews 38 interception return
    (Crosby kick), 14:50.
GIANTS – Jacobs 1 run (Tynes kick), 6:44.
PACKERS – Driver 13 pass from Rodgers
    (Crosby kick), 1:10.

THIRD QUARTER
PACKERS – G.Jennings 20 pass from Rodgers
    (Crosby kick), 9:50.
GIANTS – Nicks 4 pass from Manning
    (Tynes kick), 6:30.

FOURTH QUARTER
GIANTS – FG Tynes 50, 10:53.
PACKERS – Driver 7 pass from Rodgers
    (Crosby kick), 3:34.
GIANTS – Nicks 2 pass from Manning
    (Ware run), :58.
PACKERS – FG Crosby 30, :00.

SCORING SUMMARY

	GB	GIANTS
First downs	29	24
Total Net Yards	449	447
Rushes-yards	28-89	20-100
Passing	360	347
Punt Returns	2-6	0-0
Kickoff Returns	3-76	5-125
Interceptions Ret.	1-38	1-9
Comp-Att-Int	28-47-1	23-40-1
Sacked-Yards Lost	2-9	1-0
Punts	5-44.2	4-44.3
Fumbles-Lost	0-0	1-1
Penalties-Yards	4-30	6-55
Time of Possession	33:03	26:57

Attendance — 80,634

INDIVIDUAL STATISTICS

RUSHING
Green Bay — Rodgers 4-32, Grant 13-29,
    Saine 6-16, Kuhn 2-7, Starks 3-5.
Giants — Jacobs 8-59, Bradshaw 11-38,
    Ware 1-3.

PASSING
Green Bay — Rodgers 28-46-1-369,
    Cobb 0-1-0-0.
Giants — Manning 23-40-1-347.

RECEIVING
Green Bay — G.Jennings 7-94, Finley 6-87,
    Nelson 4-94, Driver 4-34, Saine 4-29,
    Grant 1-17, Crabtree 1-7, Quarless 1-7.
Giants — Cruz 7-119, Nicks 7-88,
    Ballard 3-47, Bradshaw 2-9, Ware 2-8,
    Beckum 1-67, Barden 1-9.

MISSED FIELD GOALS
Green Bay — Green Bay, Crosby 43 (WR).

GAME STATS
DECEMBER 4, 2011

OUT OF THE BLUE.

GAME THIRTEEN
GIANTS 37 | COWBOYS 34

WITH THEIR SEASON ON THE LINE, MANNING STEPS UP TO SAVE BIG BLUE IN BIG D

BY RALPH VACCHIANO

Eli Manning has been saving games for the Giants all year. This time he saved their season.

The Comeback Quarterback did it again when he led the Giants to their most important come-from-behind win of the season. Manning led the Giants to two touchdowns in three minutes, 14 seconds, including the go-ahead Brandon Jacobs TD run with 46 seconds remaining, to lift Big Blue over the Dallas Cowboys, 37-34.

It wasn't over, though, until the final second when Manning got a huge assist from Giants defensive end Jason Pierre-Paul, who rose up and blocked Dan Bailey's second attempt at a game-tying, 47-yard field goal. Bailey's first attempt was good, but it came after the Giants had called timeout.

When his retry failed, the Giants were officially back in first place in the NFC East.

"We've had some wild games here over the years — none probably wilder than this," Manning said after the Giants snapped their four-game losing streak. "It was a great job by our guys not getting down, not getting frustrated and continuing to believe."

They believed because, as Manning said, "We've been in these situations before." This was the fifth time this season he's led the Giants back from a fourth-quarter deficit to a win, and the 20th time he's done it in his career. It also might have been his most important since Super Bowl XLII, because had the Giants (7-6) lost, their road to the playoffs would have been nearly impossible.

Instead, they return home tied with the Cowboys (7-6) atop the division, but holding a temporary tie-breaker advantage. They are also still in play in the NFC wild-card chase, if necessary, where they trail the Detroit Lions (8-5) and the Atlanta Falcons (8-5) by one game.

Most importantly, though, they headed home with a win — a feeling they hadn't had since they won in New England on Nov. 6.

"We needed a locker-room celebration," Tom Coughlin said. "We've been starving for that. I was so happy for our players that they won. It won't be such a bad trip home."

Like most of the Giants' games this season, that wasn't clear until the final moments despite another stellar effort by Manning (27-of-47 for 400 yards, two touchdowns and one interception). As he usually is against the Cowboys, he was locked in quite a duel with Tony Romo, who passed for four touchdowns and 321

Left: Eli Manning is fired up after throwing a fourth-quarter touchdown in a big road victory in Dallas. *Evan Pinkus | AP Photo*

Above: Jason Pierre-Paul comes up huge, blocking Dan Bailey's 47-yard field goal attempt in closing seconds to secure a Giants' victory. *Sharon Ellman* | *AP Photo*

yards. For a long time, the Giants couldn't stop him or Felix Jones, who replaced the injured DeMarco Murray (broken ankle) and rushed for 106 yards.

But the Giants — who played without Ahmad Bradshaw for the entire first half because Coughlin benched him for a "violation of team rules" — matched the Cowboys score for score and were even up 22-20 heading into the fourth quarter. But Romo broke it open, first with a 74-yard pass to Laurent Robinson that set up a 6-yard touchdown pass to Miles Austin, and then — after Manning was intercepted on a screen pass that was tipped at the Cowboys' 21 — with a 50-yard touchdown pass to an uncovered Dez Bryant.

At that point, Coughlin admitted "it didn't look very good." That "historical" collapse that Justin Tuck had warned about last month seemed to be on the horizon. But on the side-lines, offensive coordinator Kevin Gilbride simply turned to Manning and said, "Hey, we need two scores. Go do it."

And Manning did, first with an 8-yard touchdown pass to tight end Jake Ballard with 3:14 remaining to cap an eight-play, 80-yard drive in 2:27. Then, after Romo overthrew a wide-open Austin on a third-down pass that would have sealed a Dallas win, Manning led a 58-yard drive that ended with Jacobs' go-ahead touchdown and a two-point conversion run by

SCORE BY QUARTERS	1	2	3	4	FINAL
Giants	5	10	7	15	37
Dallas	7	10	3	14	34

OUT OF THE BLUE:

D.J. Ware. There were still 46 seconds left on the clock, though, and the Cowboys moved quickly into Bailey's field-goal range.

His first kick was good, but Coughlin had called timeout just before the ball was snapped. That forced a re-kick and allowed Pierre-Paul to change his strategy and rush over the center instead of the guard. This time, he got through, blocking the kick and sending the Giants into a frenzy, that included a primal scream of relief and joy from co-owner John Mara up in the press box.

"We needed a play," said defensive tackle (and former Cowboy) Chris Canty. "And we had somebody rise up and make that play." ■

Above: Giants wide receiver Victor Cruz catches an Eli Manning pass and runs 74 yards for a touchdown. *David Drapkin | AP Photo*

SCORING SUMMARY

FIRST QUARTER
GIANTS – Pierre-Paul safety, 9:42.
GIANTS – FG Tynes 23, 7:07.
COWBOYS – Phillips 12 pass from Romo (Bailey kick), 2:49.

SECOND QUARTER
GIANTS – Jacobs 1 run (Tynes kick), 12:45.
COWBOYS – Robinson 9 pass from Romo (Bailey kick), 6:26.
GIANTS – FG Tynes 26, 1:03.
COWBOYS – FG Bailey 49, :15.

THIRD QUARTER
COWBOYS – FG Bailey 49, 7:42.
GIANTS – Manningham 47 pass from Manning (Tynes kick), 4:30.

FOURTH QUARTER
COWBOYS – Austin 6 pass from Romo (Bailey kick), 12:45.
COWBOYS – Bryant 50 pass from Romo (Bailey kick), 5:41.
GIANTS – Ballard 8 pass from Manning (Tynes kick), 3:14.
GIANTS – Jacobs 1 run (Ware run), :46.

SCORING SUMMARY

	GIANTS	DAL
First downs	28	23
Total Net Yards	510	444
Rushes-yards	31-110	24-139
Passing	400	305
Punt Returns	2-21	1-10
Kickoff Returns	4-74	1-25
Interceptions Ret.	0-0	1-30
Comp-Att-Int	27-47-1	21-31-0
Sacked-Yards Lost	0-0	3-16
Punts	4-44.5	3-43.7
Fumbles-Lost	0-0	1-1
Penalties-Yards	6-55	10-51
Time of Possession	34:19	25:41

Attendance — 95,952

INDIVIDUAL STATISTICS

RUSHING
Giants — Jacobs 19-101, Bradshaw 8-12, Ware 2-(minus 1), Manning 2-(minus 2).
Dallas — Jones 16-106, Murray 5-25, Austin 1-5, Fiammetta 2-3.

PASSING
Giants — Manning 27-47-1-400.
Dallas — Romo 21-31-0-321.

RECEIVING
Giants — Nicks 7-154, Cruz 7-83, Ballard 4-52, Ware 3-19, Manningham 2-62, Hynoski 2-12, Beckum 1-11, Bradshaw 1-7.
Dallas — Jones 6-31, Robinson 4-137, Austin 4-63, Witten 3-12, Bryant 1-50, Phillips 1-12, Fiammetta 1-10, Murray 1-6.

MISSED FIELD GOALS
Dallas — Bailey 47 (BK).

GAME STATS
DECEMBER 11, 2011

OUT OF THE BLUE.

THERE'S NOTHING SUPER ABOUT BEING SWEPT BY THE LOWLY REDSKINS

BY RALPH VACCHIANO

There was a simple reason why the Giants fell flat on their faces in such a critical game and again pushed themselves to the brink of elimination. It came down to one thing, according to Antrel Rolle.

And for emphasis, he pointed straight to his chest.

"If you don't got it in the heart, I don't know," Rolle said. "Washington, they're not a bad team at all. But we are 10 times better than what we showed out there on the field today."

Maybe the Giants are better, but it doesn't matter after their heartless, 23-10 loss to the already-eliminated Redskins at the Meadowlands on Sunday afternoon. It was a "hurtful loss," said Rolle, who also ripped into some of his teammates for sitting out practices during the week with minor injuries. Justin Tuck added that the loss left him "a little bit embarrassed."

It also left the Giants (7-7) facing the possibility that they could be eliminated from playoff contention on Christmas Eve.

The Giants still control their destiny - if they win their final two games they are the NFC East champs — but after the stinker of an effort they gave against Washington (5-9) that hardly seems encouraging. Their offense self-destructed for its worst performance of the season. Eli Manning, who has been red-hot all year, threw three interceptions.

And while the Giants did pick off two Rex Grossman passes, they gave up 123 rushing

Left: Hakeem Nicks can't hang onto this Eli Manning pass in another long afternoon against Washington.
Ron Antonelli | Daily News

yards and let the Redskins hold the ball for 35 minutes. They felt they came out playing with fire and intensity, but by the time the Redskins took a 10-0 lead on a 20-yard pass from Grossman to Santana Moss early in the second quarter, they could sense it all slipping away.

"I'm very disappointed in how we played," said Tom Coughlin. "I told the players that I just expected to see more. I expected to see quality, quality execution and really, quite frankly, we didn't get much of that. We didn't look like the team that played (in Dallas last) Sunday night."

Added Tuck, "I've got a big knot in my stomach right now with how we just played."

Corey Webster picked off Grossman on his flea-flicker pass on the first play of the game, but the Giants' offense couldn't get started. Manning (23-of-40, 257 yards) opened with a career-worst 0-for-6 start. Hakeem Nicks' first of three dropped passes would've been a 54-yard touchdown (he said he lost the ball in the sun).

The Redskins' 10-0 lead became 17-0 midway through the second quarter when fullback Darrel Young had a virtually uncontested 6-yard touchdown run up the middle. The Giants closed to within 17-3 at the half, but threw their momentum away when Manning was picked off by DeAngelo Hall on his first pass of the third quarter.

"We thought we could hit a few big plays," Manning said. "That's what it was going to take - a few big plays, some long touchdowns to spark our offense. They were there. We just didn't capitalize on those."

Even the Giants' last-ditch effort at another fantastic finish turned into something of a dark comedy. Trailing 23-3, Manning was picked off in the end zone early in the fourth quarter. Then the Giants got the ball back and got to the Redskins' 3 with 91/2 minutes remaining, only to have Nicks drop another touchdown pass, have an apparent D.J. Ware touchdown overturned on replay and a Nicks touchdown catch wiped out by a holding penalty on left tackle David Diehl.

Not that it mattered. Even the few fans who remained at the Meadowlands to stare at the carnage knew the Giants didn't have the energy or intensity to work their fourth-quarter magic.

"I don't feel like we had enough 'fighting mode' to come back in this game," Rolle said.

That's mind-boggling, considering what was at stake for the Giants. Now, instead of being tied for first and having a chance to lock up the NFC East on Saturday afternoon, they will be eliminated if they lose to the Jets and then the Cowboys beat the Eagles on Saturday night. The Giants can still win the division by winning out. There's even a scenario where they can lose to the Jets and still win the division. They are out of contention in the wild-card race.

"Sometimes we go out there and we play like we're coming to play football (and) sometimes we go out there and just take the field," Rolle said. "It's not good enough. Of course we have (heart). It's been proven that we have it.

Honestly, I don't know why we don't just go out there and play with it every game."∎

Above: Giants defensive end Justin Tuck.
Ron Antonelli | Daily News

SCORE BY QUARTERS	1	2	3	4	FINAL
Washington	3	14	3	3	23
Giants	0	3	0	7	10

OUT OF THE BLUE.

Above: Jason Pierre-Paul and Chris Canty celebrate a sack of Rex Grossman, but it's one of only a few highlights on this day.
Ron Antonelli | Daily News

SCORING SUMMARY

FIRST QUARTER
REDSKINS – FG Gano 36, 9:14.

SECOND QUARTER
REDSKINS – Moss 20 pass from Grossman (Gano kick), 13:42.
REDSKINS – Young 6 run (Gano kick), 7:56.
GIANTS – FG Tynes 40, :02.

THIRD QUARTER
REDSKINS – FG Gano 43, 11:49.

FOURTH QUARTER
REDSKINS – FG Gano 25, 14:57.
GIANTS – Bradshaw 3 run (Tynes kick), :33.

SCORING SUMMARY

	WASH	GIANTS
First downs	19	22
Total Net Yards	300	324
Rushes-yards	40-123	18-91
Passing	177	233
Punt Returns	1-(-2)	0-0
Kickoff Returns	3-27	4-104
Interceptions Ret.	3-52	2-0
Comp-Att-Int	15-24-2	23-40-3
Sacked-Yards Lost	1-8	3-24
Punts	2-33.0	4-49.0
Fumbles-Lost	1-0	1-0
Penalties-Yards	2-48	8-75
Time of Possession	35:00	25:00

Attendance — 78,861

INDIVIDUAL STATISTICS

RUSHING
Washington — Helu 23-53, Royster 10-36, Young 4-14, Armstrong 1-14, Paul 1-7, Grossman 1-(minus 1).
Giants — Bradshaw 10-58, Jacobs 8-33.

PASSING
Washington — Grossman 15-24-2-185.
Giants — Manning 23-40-3-257.

RECEIVING
Washington — Gaffney 6-85, Helu 3-16, Moss 2-40, Stallworth 2-35, Paulsen 1-9, Young 1-0.
Giants — Nicks 5-73, Cruz 5-44, Manningham 3-57, Bradshaw 3-21, Pascoe 2-26, Hynoski 2-13, Ballard 1-15, Barden 1-6, Ware 1-2.

MISSED FIELD GOALS
Giants — Tynes 44 (WL).

GAME STATS
DECEMBER 18, 2011

BY RALPH VACCHIANO

The laptop computer in Corey Webster's locker is filled with video of Brandon Marshall, the dangerous receiver he'll be shadowing all afternoon. It has more than that, too. It's a treasure trove of clips of the NFL's best receivers and cornerbacks. It also has clips of nearly every play Webster has ever made.

He spent the offseason studying them. He saw the good plays he quietly made all last season. He studied the awful beginning of his NFL life under his first defensive coordinator, Tim Lewis. He looked at how he played late in 2007 after his savior, Steve Spagnuolo, revived his career. He even watched himself playing in college.

So he was ready when defensive coordinator Perry Fewell came to him early this season and told him the Giants were altering their game plan: Webster was going to be locked on the No. 1 receiver.

That's when Fewell first noticed the "sparkle in his eye."

"It wasn't that Webby comes out and says, 'Hey, I'm the guy' or anything like that," Fewell says. "He doesn't beat his chest. He studies. There's that twinkle - that look like, 'I got this responsibility. I am the man.'"

A man, not a sideshow, Webster insists. There's no flash to his game. No catchy nickname. No dance. Nothing to draw attention to himself like some other cornerbacks he knows. It's why the world has hardly noticed that no team's best receiver has really hurt the Giants this season.

"Probably because I don't say crazy things," the seventh-year pro says. "Some people come out and do gimmicky stuff to get their names out there. I just go about my business like this is my job, this is what you asked me to do. I don't name myself an island."

When he opens his laptop, though, he finds that he's always been on one, locked on the opponents' top receiver as far back as he can see. He's always been "The man" and he's always had it covered, even in the days when he was in Lewis' doghouse or on Spagnuolo's bench. "Let me tell you, I've never seen me not being this player right here," Webster says. "That's all I've ever been."

In the beginning, there was confusion.

Above: Corey Webster has emerged under defensive coordinator Perry Fewell this season. *Bryan Pace | Daily News*

That's what Webster remembers most after he was drafted in the second round out of LSU in 2005. He tried to learn Lewis' defense, even though it forced him to play off the receiver when he knew he was better suited to press coverage. He tried to do what Lewis asked of him. He just was never really sure what that was. "You'd go out there and do exactly what you were supposed to do, but then come in the locker room

Above: Corey Webster, who is happy when nobody mentions his name, returns an interception against the Bills.
Robert Sabo | Daily News

and get busted," Webster says. "How do you get busted for doing what you're supposed to do? There was too much black, white and gray. We were too wishy-washy. We didn't know what was going on. I didn't like it. How can you be successful with that? If (the coach) doesn't know what's going on, how do you want me to know? Nobody knew what was going on when they walked out on the field. Everybody's got some doubt in their mind that it's not going to work."

When it didn't work, Webster says, Lewis rode him hard. Webster says now that his confidence was never shaken, though it sure looked that way on the field. "It's a different situation when you've got a coach who doesn't have faith in you," he says.

That didn't appear to change much after the unpopular Lewis was fired before the 2007 season, replaced by Spagnuolo. Two-and-a-half awful games into Spagnuolo's tenure, in Washington, Webster made a mistake on a deep pass to Santana Moss that looked like the last straw of a short career. Spagnuolo never yelled. He simply told Webster it was time to "Take a break."

Webster lost his starting job and was even inactive for two games. But Spagnuolo never lost faith. "He showed me how much I meant to him," Webster says. "He said, 'Look, you've been working hard in practice. Don't stop working.' So I kept it up. And when it was time for me he said, 'He's not rusty. He's ready to go in.' I knew when I got the opportunity that he was going to do the right thing

by me, and he did. And he put me right back on the No. 1 receiver."

Webster started his turnaround in the playoff-clinching win in Buffalo with a 34-yard interception return for a touchdown. When Sam Madison and Kevin Dockery got hurt, Spagnuolo line up Webster against the best: Tampa Bay's Joey Galloway, Dallas' Terrell Owens, Green Bay's Donald Driver and New England's Randy Moss. Webster made Galloway and Owens disappear. And while he's still kicking himself for slipping on Driver's 90-yard touchdown catch in the NFC Championship Game, Webster did make the game-turning interception in overtime. He gave up a touchdown to Moss in the Super Bowl, but also made a huge, finger-tip deflection of a Tom Brady pass on the Pats' last, desperation drive.

The way to tell how Webster's playing this season is by how little his name is heard.

"I'll measure it by this," Fewell says. "We don't call his name too much. I'd like to keep it that way - except when he gets interceptions."

The key for Webster was that he knew what he was supposed to do and he knew Fewell believed he could he do it. He saw no need to stand up and take a bow, or plant a flag on Webster Island.

"I'm playing pretty good," Webster says. "But I'm not a big talker and all that. I can fly underneath the radar. Now me, I think I'm the best. But I can be next to Revis Island and I'll just be chilling. I like what he does. I like his style of play.

"But I'm going to still go out there and try to be better than him."◾

THE GIANTS' SHOCKING SUPER SEASON

OUT OF THE BLUE

GAME FIFTEEN
GIANTS 29 | JETS 14

FOR THIS YEAR, GIANTS EARN BRAGGING RIGHTS OVER THEIR BRASHER CROSSTOWN RIVALS

BY RALPH VACCHIANO

The last straw came when the Giants arrived at the stadium on Saturday and saw all their Super Bowl logos on the wall outside their locker room covered with black curtains. After a week of listening to the Jets talk, that was the final insult.

Boy did it feel good to the Giants to tear those curtains down.

That's the first thing they did after coming off the field with their honor restored and playoff hopes saved thanks to an emotional, 29-14 win over their intra-city rivals in the Meadowlands. David Diehl, Lawrence Tynes and Zak DeOssie did the honors as soon as the game was over, but the entire Giants organization shared their joy.

"We all saw that as a sign of disrespect," Diehl said. "They've worked extremely hard to cover up our logos and the Super Bowl trophies right outside our locker room. I think all of us said, 'Hey, fine. Let them do what they want to do. But after this game, we're going to show that this is a team with a lot of pride.' "

They showed plenty of that on Saturday with a stellar performance that included five sacks and three turnovers by their revitalized defense and the first 99-yard play in franchise history on a touchdown pass from Eli Manning to Victor Cruz. It was a relentless effort worthy of their "big brother" status that the Jets had so loudly been after.

"Given all the noise that was coming out of Florham Park, it's a satisfying win," said the Giants' usually reserved co-owner, John Mara. "It kind of reinvigorates this franchise and the players."

Brandon Jacobs, who got into an argument with Rex Ryan on the field after the game, was a bit more pointed in his message to the Jets that he put so eloquently: "It's time for them to shut the f--- up."

This was about far more important things than "bragging rights" for the Giants, of course. The win literally saved their season. Had they lost they could have been eliminated from contention. Instead, they'll wake up on Christmas morning knowing they can start preparing for a winner-take-all showdown for the NFC East title with the Dallas Cowboys at MetLife Stadium on New Year's Day (8:20 p.m., Ch. 4).

But don't underestimate how much those "bragging rights" meant to this franchise and its players, especially after listening to constant trash-talking from Ryan and his players that really began three years ago when Ryan got the Jets job. Nobody

Left: Giants defensive tackle Chris Canty tackles Mark Sanchez in the end zone for a safety.
Corey Sipkin | Daily News

Above: Giants' offense, including Brandon Jacobs, left, and Ahmad Bradshaw, right, enjoy victory against the Jets.
Ken Goldfield | Daily News

SCORE BY QUARTERS	1	2	3	4	FINAL
Giants	0	10	7	12	29
Jets	7	0	0	7	14

OUT OF THE BLUE.

seemed to take it more personally than Jacobs.

Jacobs called Ryan a "disrespectful bastard" and said the coach told him to "shut the f--- up." Jacobs also called Ryan a "fat boy." And when Ryan tried to talk back to him, Jacobs said, "I told him I'd punch him in the head."

Those warm holiday wishes aside, that's exactly what the Giants (8-7) did to the Jets (8-7) with arguably their finest defensive performance of the year. Jets quarterback Mark Sanchez tried in vain to pick apart the Giants' vulnerable defense by throwing the ball 59 times. But he completed only 30, was held to 258 yards and threw two interceptions. He was also sacked five times and lost a fumble.

"Last week we practiced with more energy, more enthusiasm and greater speed (on defense) than we had in a long time, and it shocked me," Tom Coughlin said. "I said, 'Is that the same guys?' The way they practiced is the way they played. They were exceptional. Regardless of the circumstance, they kept turning the Jets offense back."

They needed it, too, because Manning struggled to find open receivers against the Jets' secondary. He completed only nine of 27 passes for 225 yards.

But he came through with two huge completions that turned the game. Late in the first half, on a thirdand10 from his own 1, he hit Cruz with a 12-yard pass that the second-year sensation turned into a 99-yard touchdown. Then late in the third quarter, he hit Cruz (three catches, 164 yards) with a 36-yarder that set up an Ahmad Bradshaw 14-yard touchdown run that gave the Giants a 17-7 lead.

The Giants had a chance to ease their way to a victory from there, but they turned the game into a nail-biter after Sanchez fumbled a snap on the Giants' 1yard line with 8:53 remaining and Giants linebacker Jacquian Williams recovered in the end zone.

Throwing on first down, Manning was picked off by Jets linebacker David Harris on the next play, and the Jets converted that into a 1-yard touchdown run by Sanchez that got them within 20-14.

But the Giants' defense wasn't finished, and defensive tackle Chris Canty sacked Sanchez in the end zone for a safety with 2:13 remaining. One failed onside kick by the Jets later and Bradshaw was running for a 19-yard touchdown that sent Jets fans scurrying for the exits.

For the Giants, though, the "bragging" had only just begun.

"Those guys in green like to do a lot of talking," Canty said. "But at the end of the day the New York football Giants talk with our football pads in between those white lines."

"We did a little talking ourselves. We're not innocent," added defensive end Justin Tuck. "But we came out and backed it up."

Yes they did, and now they still have a chance to back up all their playoff guarantees with one more big regular-season game. But that's for later. First, they needed to reassert what Diehl yelled when he tore down the curtains:

This is Giants Stadium!"■

SCORING SUMMARY

FIRST QUARTER
JETS – Baker 5 pass from Sanchez (Folk kick), 7:56.

SECOND QUARTER
GIANTS – FG Tynes 21, 11:51.
GIANTS – Cruz 99 pass from Manning (Tynes kick), 2:12.

THIRD QUARTER
GIANTS – Bradshaw 14 run (Tynes kick), :13.

FOURTH QUARTER
GIANTS – FG Tynes 36, 13:18.
JETS – Sanchez 1 run (Folk kick), 7:17.
GIANTS – Canty safety, 2:13.
GIANTS – Bradshaw 19 run (Tynes kick), 2:04.

SCORING SUMMARY

	GIANTS	JETS
First downs	11	22
Total Net Yards	332	331
Rushes-yards	26-115	25-105
Passing	217	226
Punt Returns	3-7	4-74
Kickoff Returns	3-77	5-110
Interceptions Ret.	2-47	1-20
Comp-Att-Int	9-27-1	30-59-2
Sacked-Yards Lost	2-8	5-32
Punts	9-43.4	9-42.1
Fumbles-Lost	0-0	1-1
Penalties-Yards	5-45	10-95
Time of Possession	23:54	36:06

Attendance — 79,088

INDIVIDUAL STATISTICS

RUSHING
Giants — Bradshaw 15-54, Jacobs 7-42, Ware 3-20, Manning 1-(minus 1).
Jets — Greene 14-58, Tomlinson 5-29, Sanchez 4-13, Kerley 1-6, Holmes 1-(minus 1).

PASSING
Giants — Manning 9-27-1-225.
Jets — Sanchez 30-59-2-258.

RECEIVING
Giants — Cruz 3-164, Nicks 1-20, Jacobs 1-13, D.Thomas 1-11, Bradshaw 1-8, Ware 1-5, Barden 1-4.
Jets — Keller 8-77, Tomlinson 6-36, Kerley 5-36, Holmes 4-50, Burress 3-34, Greene 3-20, Baker 1-5.

MISSED FIELD GOALS
Jets — Folk 44 (WR).

JACOBS

GAME SIXTEEN
GIANTS 31 | COWBOYS 14

BIG PLAYS BY ELI MANNING & VICTOR CRUZ HELP GIANTS CLINCH NFC EAST CROWN

BY RALPH VACCHIANO

This time there was no collapse. This time the Giants finished what they started.

Even in the frightening moments on Sunday night when they seemed to be on the brink of blowing a three-touchdown lead, the Giants found a way to once again save their season. They rode the big plays of Eli Manning and Victor Cruz and the revived play of their defense to beat the Cowboys, 31-14, in a winner-take-all showdown at the Meadowlands.

Then they all breathed a huge sigh of relief and celebrated their NFC East championship and their first trip to the playoffs since 2008.

"There were some times tonight when it was a little nerve-wracking," said Tom Coughlin. "But we straightened it around and finished the game the way we wanted to finish it — finished the regular season the way we wanted to finish it — and created an opportunity for ourselves to be in the playoffs now."

The opportunity begins on Sunday at 1 p.m. when the Giants (9-7) play host to the Atlanta Falcons (10-6) in the wild-card round, and true to the motto they've adopted, the Giants are "all in" for the postseason run. Their rousing victory over the Jets and Cowboys the last two weeks have them riding a wave of confidence they think can carry them

Above: Osi Umenyiora celebrates after a sack.
Ron Antonelli | Daily News

Left: Brandon Jacobs has a rough afternoon with just 57 yards, but his teammates pick him up for a victory.
Robert Sabo | Daily News

THE GIANTS' SHOCKING SUPER SEASON

75

Above: The Giants race off the field at halftime with a 21-0 lead over the rival Cowboys. *Corey Sipkin* | *Daily News*

deep into the winter.

"I wouldn't want to face the New York Giants right now," said running back Brandon Jacobs. "It's going to be tough to beat us in the playoffs."

Added defensive end Justin Tuck: "We're capable of winning the Super Bowl."

After the way they played on Sunday night, who could argue? Eli Manning again torched the Cowboys, this time for 346 yards and three touchdowns, including a jolting, 74-yarder to Victor Cruz that got the party started in the first quarter. Cruz, a second alternate on the NFC Pro Bowl team, ended up with six catches for 178 yards and was a big part in the Giants taking a 21-0 halftime lead.

That was their largest lead since last Dec. 19 when they famously blew a 21-point lead at home against the Eagles — a fact that surely

had to be on everyone's mind when the Cowboys got going in the second half. Despite his injured right hand, Cowboys quarterback Tony Romo (29-for-37, 289 yards) struck quickly in the third quarter, with a 94-yard drive that ended with a 34-yard pass to Laurent Robinson, cutting the deficit to 21-7.

And the Cowboys kept coming. Antrel Rolle came up with an interception. Then early in the fourth quarter, linebacker Michael Boley and defensive end Jason Pierre-Paul stopped Romo on a fourth-and-1 sneak attempt at the Giants' 10. Yet Romo — with the help of a 15-yard personal foul on Giants receiver Devin Thomas on a punt return — rallied to hit Robinson with a 6-yard touchdown pass with 10:15 remaining.

Suddenly, the Giants only had a seven-point lead.

Nervous? You bet. Right up until the nine-

SCORE BY QUARTERS	1	2	3	4	FINAL
Dallas	0	0	7	7	14
Giants	7	14	0	10	31

OUT OF THE BLUE.

Above: Eli Manning calls signals at the line of scrimmage.
Ron Antonelli | Daily News

Above: Tom Coughlin welcomes his team to the sideline after an Ahmad Bradshaw touchdown.
Corey Sipkin | Daily News

minute mark. That's when Manning, on a third-and-7 from the Giants' 28, spun out of trouble, reset and fired a Super Bowl-like pass down the field to a well-covered Cruz. The receiver jumped up with Cowboys cornerback Orlando Scandrick on his back and came down with a 44-yard catch.

"That catch was a boost, I'll tell you that," said guard Chris Snee. "Times were tough. We weren't doing very well."

"It just seems like whenever we need a big play," Tuck added of Cruz, "he's stepped up and been that guy."

The play was huge and so was his 20-yard catch two plays later that got the Giants in range for a 28-yard Lawrence Tynes field goal that gave them a 24-14 lead. One three-and-out by the Cowboys later and Manning was sealing the deal with a 4-yard touchdown pass to Hakeem Nicks.

Then came Coughlin's Gatorade shower and the long-awaited celebration was on.

"We were long overdue for this moment and this opportunity," Rolle said. "I think everyone threw in all their poker chips. We were all in."

They had to be considering the way this season had gone. They had blown almost all of their surprising 6-2 start and spent the last two weeks on the brink of elimination, leading to speculation that Coughlin was once again in danger of being fired. But the players rallied behind him to earn the playoff berth that GM Jerry Reese had promised back in the summer, when everyone already seemed to be counting the Giants out.

"NFC East champions," Coughlin said. "That's a great thing to hear." ∎

SCORING SUMMARY

FIRST QUARTER
GIANTS – Cruz 74 pass from Manning (Tynes kick), 4:57.

SECOND QUARTER
GIANTS – Bradshaw 5 run (Tynes kick), 13:27.
GIANTS – Bradshaw 10 pass from Manning (Tynes kick), 1:09.

THIRD QUARTER
COWBOYS – Robinson 34 pass from Romo (Bailey kick), 6:54.

FOURTH QUARTER
COWBOYS – Robinson 6 pass from Romo (Bailey kick), 10:15.
GIANTS –FG Tynes 28, 5:45.
GIANTS –Nicks 4 pass from Manning (Tynes kick), 3:41.

SCORING SUMMARY

	DAL	GIANTS
First downs	19	20
Total Net Yards	300	437
Rushes-yards	16-49	31-106
Passing	251	331
Punt Returns	3-17	3-1
Kickoff Returns	6-127	3-66
Interceptions Ret.	0-0	1-(-1)
Comp-Att-Int	29-37-1	24-33-0
Sacked-Yards Lost	6-38	2-15
Punts	6-42.3	4-40.3
Fumbles-Lost	2-1	2-0
Penalties-Yards	7-43	3-28
Time of Possession	25:27	34:33

Attendance — 81,077

INDIVIDUAL STATISTICS

RUSHING
Dallas — F.Jones 11-30, Morris 3-16, Romo 2-3.
Giants — Bradshaw 16-57, Ware 2-19, Jacobs 7-16, Manning 6-14.

PASSING
Dallas — Romo 29-37-1-289.
Giants — Manning 24-33-0-346.

RECEIVING
Dallas — Witten 7-69, F.Jones 7-47, Bryant 6-70, Robinson 4-61, Austin 2-20, Fiammetta 1-14, Bennett 1-5, Morris 1-3.
Giants — Cruz 6-178, Nicks 5-76, Hynoski 4-31, Bradshaw 3-12, Pascoe 2-14, Beckum 2-13, D.Thomas 1-14, Ware 1-8.

MISSED FIELD GOALS
Dallas — Bailey 52 (WL).
Giants — Tynes 40 (WR).

GAME STATS
JANUARY 1, 2012

GIANTS CATCH

Linval Joseph celebrates after a tackle in the Wild Card game against Atlanta. *Ron Antonelli | Daily News*

OUT OF THE BLUE.

WILD CARD
GIANTS 24 | FALCONS 2

THIS TIME, DEFENSE DOMINATES FOR GIANTS AS ELI & CO. ARE ALLOWED A RARE EASY GAME

BY RALPH VACCHIANO

The Giants were only supposed to go as far as Eli Manning could carry them this season. But when the playoffs began, the defense showed it won't just be along for the ride.

That once-beleaguered unit turned back the clock on Sunday afternoon and gave a dominating performance reminiscent of some of the greatest games in the Giants' storied playoff past. The defense pitched a virtual shutout, smothering the Atlanta Falcons 24-2 in a wild-card playoff game, giving the Giants their first postseason win in the Meadowlands in nearly 11 years.

"We played outstanding defense and that set the tone for everything else that happened in the game," Tom Coughlin said. "And if we can continue to play defense like that, we can make ourselves heard in this tournament."

Their next chance to make noise will come next Sunday in Green Bay, where as nine-point underdogs they'll get the rematch with the Packers (15-1) they've been craving

Above: Giants fans don't have a lot of love for anybody named Ryan. *Robert Sabo | Daily News*

Left: Osi Umenyiora sacks Falcons QB Matt Ryan to close out a dominant performance by the Giants defense. *Ron Antonelli | Daily News*

since they lost to them on a last-second field goal back on Dec. 4. That feels like years ago, though, to this revitalized defense.

That's why Jason Pierre-Paul said: "We know it's one and done (and) we aren't going to let that happen. We're going to go out there and we're going to walk away with a win."

The confidence is understandable, coming off what Justin Tuck described as "probably our best effort this year" on defense. The Giants (10-7) gave up only 247 total yards. They turned Falcons running back Michael Turner (15 carries, 41 yards) into an afterthought. And they came up with two huge stops on fourth-and-1 quarterback sneaks deep in their own territory.

In fact, the only points the Falcons got came off a second-quarter safety when Eli Manning was flagged for intentional grounding in the end zone. Other than that, the Giants' offense was actually pretty good. In fact, the balanced performance of this pass-happy group even left Coughlin "surprised." The Giants rushed for a season-high 172 yards and Manning threw for 277 yards and three touchdowns most of which came in the second half.

They were able to do that, though, because the defense set the tone against a Falcons offense that thought it could bully its way to a win. The two key moments were nearly identical: a fourth-and-inches for the Falcons at the Giants' 24 on the first play of the second quarter, and another fourth-and-inches from the Giants' 21 late in the third. Both times the Falcons tried a simple quarterback sneak with Matt Ryan.

That "was rude," defensive end Osi Umenyiora said. But both times the Giants' revitalized defense stopped him cold.

"We made a statement that you can't run the ball on us," Pierre-Paul said. "Fourth-and-one, you might as well kick a

Right: Eli Manning enjoys another TD pass, this time to Mario Manningham in the fourth quarter of a Wild Card rout of the Falcons.
Andrew Theodorakis I *Daily News*

OUT OF THE BLUE.

Above: Brandon Jacobs bulls his way for extra yardage as the Giants prove to be way too much for Atlanta.
Corey Sipkin | Daily News

field goal. I feel like it's disrespectful for them to go for it, but you see the outcome."

"You can go through all the fancy Xs and Os, but fourth-and-1 is really all about heart," added defensive tackle Chris Canty. "It's all about heart. It's all about want-to. And at the end of the day we wanted it more than they did."

After the first fourth-and-1, the Falcons actually bounced back. Three plays later, with the Giants facing a second-and-19 from their own 13, Atlanta safety James Sanders came blitzing by Giants right tackle Kareem McKenzie and pressured Manning. But Manning intentionally grounded the ball just as he stepped back into the end zone, giving the Falcons a safety and a 2-0 lead.

Only then did the Giants' offense get going. On their next drive the Giants got a 34-yard run from Brandon Jacobs (14 carries, 92 yards), who followed that a few plays later by spinning his way to a first down on the

Giants' own fourth-and-inches. Manning then hit Hakeem Nicks (6 catches, 115 yards, 2 touchdowns) for a 4-yard pass that amazingly was the first playoff touchdown at home in the Manning/Coughlin Era.

Manning and Nicks would hook up again in the second half on a short pass about five yards over the middle that Nicks caught, turned upfield, split five defenders and turned into a 72-yard touchdown. He celebrated by doing the "Dirty Bird" dance in the end zone as the Giants, with 2:44 remaining in the third quarter, had a 17-2 lead.

That was insurmountable the way the Giants' defense was playing.

"We went out there and we put the stamp on it," said safety Antrel Rolle. "This is what I've been waiting for. (And) we still can get better."

"It's about heart," Umenyiora added. "We weren't going to take nothing from nobody. We weren't going to get pushed around. I think we went out there and it showed."■

BY MIKE LUPICA

THIS REALLY WAS Giants Stadium now, a game out of the past and from across the parking lot in the Meadowlands, from all the big Sundays when the old Giants beat you with defense. They were up all around us where we were sitting on the Giants side of this new stadium, waving their towels, wanting this to be like the last home playoff game the Giants had won, a long time ago, an NFC Championship Game against the Vikings 11 years ago, when the Vikings got shut out, when the Giants wouldn't give the Vikings an inch that day.

So now they were up at the new Stadium, on this day when the Giants played like the old Giants, Giants fans telling this defense, Tom Coughlin's, Perry Fewell's, not to give Matt Ryan and the Falcons an inch on another fourth down.

They had stopped Ryan on another fourth down in the first half. The place yelled its head off for the Giants to do it again. This was before Eli would throw it to Hakeem Nicks — Elite Manning, taking his team to the Elite Eight of pro football on this day — and before he'd throw another one to Mario Manningham. It was still only 10-2 for the Giants, still a long way from Lambeau Field, from "keeping the dream alive," as Coughlin would say when it was over.

A long way from another shot at the Green Bay Packers.

Fourth-and-inches at MetLife Stadium. Mike Smith, the completely overmatched Falcons coach, was sure helping now in this crazy, loud moment, going with an empty backfield, telling everybody in the place that Ryan was going to try another sneak, doing everything but announcing that over the P.A. system. As if anybody would have heard in the Giants part of Jersey.

Give him nothing, that's what they were saying on this day when the only points the Falcons were going to get off the Giants would come on a first-half safety, Eli throwing it to nobody out of the end zone. Pitch the same kind of defensive shutout the Giants had pitched the last time the Giants won a playoff game in Jersey, 41-0 against the Vikings.

Ryan took the snap and it was as if all the guys on the defensive line stopped him at once, as if they were all the

Above: The Giants stop Atlanta not once, but twice on 4th-and-1 situations. *Robert Sabo | Daily News*

SCORE BY QUARTERS	1	2	3	4	FINAL
Atlanta	0	2	0	0	2
Giants	0	7	10	7	24

OUT OF THE BLUE

guys on all the lines who ever made a big stop for the Giants in a big game. Ryan never got near the line or the first down and the place exploded all over again, the white flags maybe looking to the Falcons as if they were being told to surrender.

Before you knew it, Eli had it to Nicks over the middle and Nicks was running away from what looked like about six white uniforms, the kind of play Victor Cruz has been making lately, and it was 17-2 now for the Giants, and it was over.

"If we continue to play (defense)," Coughlin said in his interview, "we have a chance to be heard in the tournament."

They have been heard already. The Giants have beaten the Jets in a knockout game and beaten the Cowboys and beaten the Falcons 24-2. It has been a long time between home playoff victories, it sure has, but they are some bookends, aren't they? This time they go to Lambeau, get another shot at Aaron Rodgers and the Packers. The last time that happened in the postseason, the Packers were the No. 1 seed in the NFC and it was the NFC Championship Game and Lawrence Tynes finally kicked one in overtime on one of the coldest football nights ever and the Giants went to Glendale.

So here come the Giants again, playing their best football of this season, the best football any Giants team has played since Plaxico Burress turned into Wyatt Earp when the Giants were trying to win two Super Bowls in a row. Eli was great again Sunday, the Giants ran the ball better than they have all season. And the defense gave the Falcons nothing. Would not give them an inch.

And so this is all the season you ever could have wanted in the preseason, when it was the Jets who were supposed to be making the big moves, when it seemed like half the Giants were hurt and they were supposed to finish third in the NFC East. When they were discussed as if they were the JV team at MetLife Stadium. Only now they go back to Lambeau, they give us another Giants-Packers game in January, they try to beat a 15-1 Packers team that only beat them a field goal at MetLife Stadium earlier in the season because they had the ball last.

Maybe this Giants team isn't as good as the one that beat Brett Favre in that overtime game. But Eli is a better player than he was then, and he has better guys to whom to throw it, and all of a sudden nobody in the sport wants to go against Jason Pierre-Paul and Justin Tuck and Chris Canty and the rest of them up front, all the guys they kept running at Matt Ryan and the Falcons on Sunday.

But again: This is all the season you could have wanted in September, all the chance. Or even all the chance you could have wanted after the Giants lost to the Redskins a few weeks ago and were 7-7, that close to next season. Like they were half a yard away. Like it was fourth down against them.

They go home if they lose to the Cowboys last Sunday night, maybe go home if those fourth-down plays go against them Sunday. Instead they go to Lambeau. Give them an inch and they don't just take a mile. Four years later, they try to take the Packers again in January.■

Above: Osi Umenyiora and Big Blue 'D' are flying high against the Falcons.
Corey Sipkin | Daily News

SCORING SUMMARY

SECOND QUARTER
FALCONS – Team safety, 13:44.
GIANTS – Nicks 4 pass from Manning (Tynes kick), 2:47.

THIRD QUARTER
GIANTS – FG Tynes 22, 7:51.
GIANTS – Nicks 72 pass from Manning (Tynes kick), 2:44.

FOURTH QUARTER
GIANTS – Manningham 27 pass from Manning (Tynes kick), 9:55.

SCORING SUMMARY

	ATL	GIANTS
First downs	14	19
Total Net Yards	247	442
Rushes-yards	21-64	31-172
Passing	183	270
Punt Returns	0-0	5-28
Kickoff Returns	4-98	1-27
Interceptions Ret.	0-0	0-0
Comp-Att-Int	24-41-0	23-32-0
Sacked-Yards Lost	2-16	1-7
Punts	7-46.0	4-45.8
Fumbles-Lost	0-0	0-0
Penalties-Yards	3-15	7-73
Time of Possession	25:26	34:34

Attendance — 79,909

INDIVIDUAL STATISTICS

RUSHING
Atlanta — Turner 15-41, Jones 1-13, Snelling 2-7, Ryan 3-3.
Giants — Jacobs 14-92, Bradshaw 14-63, Manning 2-13, Ware 1-4.

PASSING
Atlanta — Ryan 24-41-0-199.
Giants — Manning 23-32-0-277.

RECEIVING
Atlanta — Jones 7-64, White 5-52, Gonzalez 4-44, Rodgers 4-18, Snelling 2-9, Douglas 1-7, Turner 1-5.
Giants — Nicks 6-115, Bradshaw 5-22, Manningham 4-68, Cruz 2-28, Ballard 2-16, Jacobs 2-8, Ware 1-13, Beckum 1-7.

MISSED FIELD GOALS
Giants — Tynes 32 (WR).

GAME STATS
JANUARY 8, 2012

OUT OF THE BLUE.

DIVISIONAL
GIANTS 37 | PACKERS 20

GIANTS TURN BACK SUPER BOWL CHAMP PACKERS, TAKE MOMENTUM & THEIR HEARTS TO SAN FRANCISCO

BY RALPH VACCHIANO

The Giants were hounded and haunted by two losses this season, two games they let slip away against two of the best teams in the NFC.

Sunday night, they got their revenge against the Green Bay Packers. Next up: Settling the score against the San Francisco 49ers in the NFC Championship Game in six days.

The Giants are a team "oozing with confidence right now," in the words of defensive end Justin Tuck, after their improbable run continued with a convincing 37-20 win over the defending Super Bowl champion Green Bay Packers in an NFC divisional playoff game at frigid Lambeau Field. The Giants shocked the Packers on their famed frozen tundra for the second time in four years.

Then again, maybe "shocked" isn't the right word.

"I'm not surprised," said safety Antrel Rolle. "I said 'We'll see them again.' We saw them again. This is the outcome."

The outcome was nothing like their 38-35 loss to the Packers they suffered at the Meadowlands on Dec. 4, just like the Giants don't expect their trip to San Francisco to end the way it did when they lost, 27-20, out there back on Nov. 13. That game ended with a potential game-tying touchdown pass from Eli Manning getting batted down at the line of scrimmage in the final seconds.

The Giants flew home that night dreaming of a rematch — and they couldn't have asked for a better scenario than to face them again with a Super Bowl XLVI berth on the line.

"We wanted this real bad," said linebacker

Above: Kenny Phillips does his version of the Lambeau Leap with Giants fans who trekked to Green Bay. *Ron Antonelli | Daily News*

Left: Hakeem Nicks continues his dominant playoff performance with this 66-yard TD catch, one of seven receptions on the day. *Corey Sipkin | Daily News*

Justin Tuck tries to remove Aaron Rodgers' head from his body as Osi Umenyiora is there for moral support. The Giants harassed the Pro Bowl quarterback all afternoon. *Ron Antonelli | Daily News*

OUT OF THE BLUE:

Above: Michael Boley sacks Aaron Rodgers, one of four Giant takedowns on the day.   *Ron Antonelli* | *Daily News*

Mathias Kiwanuka. "Real bad. They make movies about stories like this. "

They sure looked that way Sunday against a Packers team that had won 21 of its last 22 games, including 15 of 16 this season. But the Giants (11-7) always felt the Packers were vulnerable, especially on defense. Manning proved the point by completing 21 of 33 passes for 330 yards and three touchdowns, despite wind chills down in the teens. He completed seven of those passes for 165 yards and two touchdowns to receiver Hakeem Nicks.

And both of Nicks' touchdowns were huge. The first was a 66-yard score in the first quarter that set the tone for the Giants when he bounced off Packers safety Charlie Peprah near midfield before outracing the defense the rest of the way. That gave the Giants an early

10-3 lead, before the Packers tied it on an 8-yard touchdown pass from Aaron Rodgers to John Kuhn in the second quarter.

The killer play came at the end of the half. The sequence started with a third-down sack by Michael Boley that gave the Giants the ball back with 41 seconds to go. Then on third-and-1, Ahmad Bradshaw took off on a long, side-to-side, 23-yard run and got out of bounds with six seconds to go.

Then, instead of trying a 54-yard field goal, Coughlin called for "Flood Tip" - the Giants' version of the Hail Mary. And it worked. Manning heaved a 37-yard pass into the end zone, where Nicks made a leaping, David Tyree-like catch, pinning the ball against his helmet for a touchdown to give the Giants a stunning, 20-10 lead.

"To see that, I think it's one or two times a

Above: Eli Manning's prayer is answered as Hakeem Nicks snares a Hail Mary touchdown to end the first half.
Ron Antonelli | Daily News

year that play is completed," Tom Coughlin said. "Fortunately for us it was completed tonight."

"It's one of the few that I have thrown up and it was the first one that was ever caught," said Manning. "It gave us all the momentum going into halftime."

It also gave them an insurmountable lead the way the Giants' revitalized defense was playing. Rodgers completed 26 of 46 passes for 246 yards, but he was sacked four times and completed only one pass all game for longer than 20 yards.

And the Giants' defense forced four turnovers, too. Osi Umenyiora (two sacks) forced a Rodgers fumble on the opening drive of the second half. Safety Kenny Phillips forced a fumble by Packers running back Ryan Grant in the fourth quarter that Chase Blackburn picked up and returned to the

Packers' 4. When Manning followed that with a 4-yard touchdown pass to Mario Manningham, the Giants were up 30-13 with just 6:48 left in the game.

By then, it was clear the Packers and their fans were stunned. But maybe they shouldn't have been. After all, Jason Pierre-Paul guaranteed this victory and nobody on the Giants disagreed.

"We told you all, man," Tuck said. "We know what we have in this room."

"I think we're a dangerous team," Coughlin added. "I like where we are. I like our attitude. I like the way we're playing."

Now the Giants are one game away from proving that they're the best team at least in the NFC.

"It's a rematch that we wanted," Kiwanuka added. "We earned it. But now we've got to go out there and prove it."■

THE GIANTS' SHOCKING SUPER SEASON

BY MIKE LUPICA

WHATEVER HAPPENS IN San Francisco next Sunday, whether the Giants keep Tom Coughlin's dream and their belief in themselves alive and make it back to another Super Bowl, this victory, this new one over the Packers Sunday night at old Lambeau Field, is as great as the Giants have ever had at this time of year. They did it to the 15-1 Packers in Green Bay the way they did it to the 18-0 Patriots in that Super Bowl four years ago. So now they have laid out two of the best seasons in football history, knocked them out cold.

And Eli Manning has beaten two of the best quarterbacks of this time in football - Tom Brady, Aaron Rodgers - straight up. It is because Eli has become one of those quarterbacks, in front of our eyes. Better now than when he won a Super Bowl four years ago. Better by a lot.

"He has been a great player this season," his father Archie said in a soft voice when it was over, a 37-20 win for the Giants that really should have been 37-6 at Lambeau. "So many great quarterbacks in this league right now. I'm just so glad my boy is in the mix."

Then Eli's dad looked around the crowded hallway outside the interview room, down from the Giants' locker room, standing next to his wife Olivia, and smiled and said, "I feel like I was standing in this exact same spot four years ago."

Four years ago Eli was better than Brett Favre in Green Bay, in an overtime NFC Championship Game, went from there to the Super Bowl, outplayed Brady and beat the Patriots. Sunday he was better than Rodgers, by a lot, as the Giants gave Rodgers and the Packers a beating and a beatdown at Lambeau.

So Eli and the Giants come in here four years later and do it again to the Packers. They were 7-7 a month ago and that close to being out of the playoffs and now they are another win away from another Super Bowl.

"We are," Tom Coughlin said, "a dangerous team."

They did it with defense this time, did it with

Right: Eli Manning at the line.
Ron Antonelli | Daily News

92

OUT OF THE BLUE

poise and talent and leadership of Eli Manning. Once, a quarter-century ago, Phil Simms threw nearly a perfect game in a Super Bowl against the Broncos. Other than that, no Giant quarterback has ever played a better game at this time of year than Eli did Sunday in Green Bay.

The Giants got ahead by 10 points at halftime when Eli threw a Hail Mary to Hakeem Nicks — he had already gone for 66 yards and a score by then — in the left corner of the end zone. Jump ball. Nicks jumped higher and even gave you a little David Tyree, the ball against his helmet for a moment, and all of a sudden a 13-10 Giants lead became 20-10. And in that moment at Lambeau, you knew it wasn't the Packers' season. They were just another team making mistakes against the Giants, another team in green.

Like they'd turned into the Jets.

Eli was the MVP of the Super Bowl once. Beat the Cowboys on the road in the playoffs that year, beat the Packers, took his team down the field to beat the 18-0 Patriots. But you have to know that he was never better than he was Sunday night in Green Bay, 21-for-33 and 330 yards and two touchdowns to Nicks and one to Mario Manningham.

He did this in one of the most famous theaters in his sport. Against a quarterback, Rodgers, who had been the best player in his sport for more than 20 games going back to last season. Against the defending champions of the world. The Giants were better Sunday night, in every phase of the game. They played against 15-1 the way they did against 18-0 four years ago.

"My son isn't afraid," Archie Manning said. "He's not afraid and he makes sure his team isn't afraid."

The defense was tremendous Sunday, and caused turnovers and pressured Rodgers and turned him into just

Left: Victor Cruz tries to Lambeau Leapfrog teammate Hakeem Nicks after another Giants score. *Corey Sipkin | Daily News*

Above: Ahmad Bradshaw runs to daylight as the Giants dethrone the Super Bowl champions. *Ron Antonelli | Daily News*

SCORE BY QUARTERS	1	2	3	4	FINAL
Giants	10	10	0	17	37
Green Bay	3	7	3	7	20

OUT OF THE BLUE:

another player on this day when the Packers became just another team, a team that never looked as good at Lambeau as the Giants did. Who beat Green Bay now and don't have to go to New Orleans to play the Saints, who ruined them during the regular season. The Giants go to San Francisco to get all the chance they ever could have wanted to go play another Super Bowl.

They won Sunday the way they have won all year, by putting the ball in Eli's hands, asking him to make the kind of plays he has made since September when his team needed him to do that. And when he needed to make one more third down throw in the fourth quarter, when he needed a first down to really put this game away — before the whole thing turned into a jailbreak at the very end — he stepped up in the pocket again and threw it to Victor Cruz. One more time on this day, you did not believe that the Packers could stop Eli Manning, this day when he was the best quarterback in the place by a lot.

"I never completed (a Hail Mary) before," Eli said when it was over. But it was that kind of day for him in Green Bay, for his team, here they come again in January, thinking anything is possible for them. Again.

It wasn't supposed to happen this way again in Lambeau. Come on? Against 15-1? You are only supposed to get one magic, underdog night in a magic football place like this. You are only supposed to make one run like the one the Giants made four years ago, all the way through the Super Bowl. Maybe not. ∎

Above: Mario Manningham gives the Giants a 30-13 lead in the fourth quarter with a 4-yard touchdown catch.
Corey Sipkin | Daily News

SCORING SUMMARY

FIRST QUARTER
GIANTS – FG Tynes 31, 8:33.
PACKERS – FG Crosby 47, 5:33.
GIANTS – Nicks 66 pass from Manning (Tynes kick), 3:47.

SECOND QUARTER
PACKERS – Kuhn 8 pass from Rodgers (Crosby kick), 14:54.
GIANTS – FG Tynes 23, 1:51.
GIANTS – Nicks 37 pass from Manning (Tynes kick), :00.

THIRD QUARTER
PACKERS – FG Crosby 35, 3:50.

FOURTH QUARTER
GIANTS – FG Tynes 35, 7:48.
GIANTS – Manningham 4 pass from Manning (Tynes kick), 6:48.
PACKERS – Driver 16 pass from Rodgers (Crosby kick), 4:46.
GIANTS – Jacobs 14 run (Tynes kick), 2:36.

SCORING SUMMARY

	GIANTS	GB
First downs	19	25
Total Net Yards	420	388
Rushes-yards	27-95	23-147
Passing	325	241
Punt Returns	0-0	1-16
Kickoff Returns	1-4	4-94
Interceptions Ret.	1-0	1-12
Comp-Att-Int	21-33-1	26-46-1
Sacked-Yards Lost	1-5	4-23
Punts	2-48.0	2-39.5
Fumbles-Lost	0-0	3-3
Penalties-Yards	3-30	3-20
Time of Possession	29:35	30:25

Attendance — 72,080

INDIVIDUAL STATISTICS

RUSHING
Giants — Bradshaw 12-63, Jacobs 9-22, Manning 4-10, Ware 2-0.
Green Bay — Rodgers 7-66, Starks 6-43, Grant 8-33, Saine 1-3, Kuhn 1-2.

PASSING
Giants — Manning 21-33-1-330.
Green Bay — Rodgers 26-46-1-264.

RECEIVING
Giants — Nicks 7-165, Cruz 5-74, Manningham 3-31, Bradshaw 3-21, Beckum 2-22, Ballard 1-17.
Green Bay — G.Jennings 4-40, Finley 4-37, Starks 4-24, Driver 3-45, Nelson 3-39, Cobb 3-38, Grant 3-17, J.Jones 1-16, Kuhn 1-8.

MISSED FIELD GOALS
Giants — Tynes 40 (BK).

GAME STATS
JANUARY 15, 2012

TOM COUGHLIN

BY RALPH VACCHIANO

It was two years of dissension and confusion for the Giants with Ray Handley as their coach and the organization desperately needed a return to the discipline and structure that allowed them to win two Super Bowls with Bill Parcells.

So, the first call following the 1992 season went to Boston College head coach Tom Coughlin, a Giants assistant from 1988-90.

"No," he said.

The Giants were shocked.

Coughlin had been at BC for just two years, the season didn't end the way he wanted and he elected to stay. It would take 11 years for him to get another chance at the job he obviously loves. But first he went to Jacksonville just one year after turning down the Giants to coach and have total control over the expansion Jaguars. He felt better about leaving BC then because things had turned around when the Eagles beat Notre Dame that season.

The Giants instead hired Dan Reeves after second-choice Dave Wannstedt chose the Bears over the Giants. Reeves lasted four years and was fired after just one playoff appearance. Jim Fassel lasted seven years with three playoff appearances and one Super Bowl appearance before he was fired after the 2003 season. Coughlin was fired by the Jaguars after the 2002 season and this time very much wanted the Giants job.

Did he ever think he would get a second chance?

"No, that wasn't any thought that I had," he said.

Staying at BC was an easy decision at the time, Coughlin said, "although any time the New York Giants would call, there isn't any question my heart would beat a little bit faster."

Back in 1993, John Mara remembered the team was "pretty disappointed, pretty surprised," that Coughlin turned them down. The Giants clearly didn't hold that against him after they fired Fassel.

"He had success in Jacksonville. I never thought we would ever have an opportunity to get him," Mara said. "But in this league, things have a funny way of working out sometimes. Coaches go from team to team, then all of a sudden, they are back with you."

Coughlin won the Super Bowl in his fourth year with the Giants and is back in his eighth. Parcells

Above: Tom Coughlin had a lot to smile about during the final month of the season. *Robert Sabo* | *Daily News*

won it in his fourth and then his eighth and final season with the Giants. Coughlin is from the Parcells coaching tree and is as close in philosophy to Parcells as any coach the Giants have had since Parcells left.

He had more ups and downs than Parcells and nearly was fired after the 2006 season. He won the Super Bowl the next year. He had three disappointing seasons after the Super Bowl and was in danger again after the Giants turned their 6-2 start into 6-6 and then 7-7. But they won their last two games against the Jets and Cowboys to win the NFC East and then getting red-hot in the playoffs.

Parcells, Reeves and Fassel, three of the four coaches who preceded Coughlin, talked about the job he has done with the Giants. Handley has not spoken to the media since his reign of error came to an end.

OUT OF THE BLUE.

Above: Tom Coughlin has loosened up some as the years have gone on and his team responded with a dominant playoffs.
Corey Sipkin | Daily News

"Tom is his own guy. I've said that 100 times," Parcells said. "He believes in a lot of sound football principles. He gives players a good design, gets them to play hard, believes in developing players. Quite obviously, he knows how to win."

Reeves had no previous ties to the Giants when he was hired, although he was a finalist for the Giants job in 1979 when he was an assistant with the Cowboys. But GM George Young picked Ray Perkins, who was an assistant with the Chargers. Young reluctantly hired Reeves in 1993 - he was concerned he could not adapt to just coaching without total control. Ultimately, Young was right.

Reeves is impressed with what Coughlin has accomplished. "It's unbelievable what he has done," Reeves said. "He's won a world championship. It doesn't hurt that you've got a good quarterback. They run the ball, they are a tough, hard-nosed team."

As a head coach, Reeves lost three Super Bowls with the Broncos and one with the Falcons and played or was an assistant coach in five with the Cowboys. Although he didn't get to one with the Giants, he does feel an attachment to the Giants.

"I love the Maras and the Tisches. They were great people to work for," he said. "I'm glad to see their success."

Fassel, who was an assistant coach under Handley before replacing Reeves in 2007, said "It's hard for me to root for any team because I've got friends everywhere, but at the end of the day, my heart is in New York."

The Giants have made it to the Super Bowl with Coughlin despite being 10-6 and 9-7 in the regular season. They join the 1979 Rams and the 2008 Cardinals as the only 9-7 teams to make it to the Super Bowl. "A team doesn't have to go into the Super Bowl 15-1 or 14-2," Fassel said." It's who gets hot and they got hot. At the end of the day, take your hat off to Tom Coughlin. He got that team focused."

Coughlin has given the Giants exactly what they wanted. He does things the Giant Way. He has come to epitomize what a Giants coach should be all about.

"I think he does," Mara said. "Too many people make too much of the fact he brings discipline. That's what we were looking for. A guy who is that dedicated and that hard-working and didn't care about image and doing TV commercials. A guy who was devoted to the Xs and Os. And that's what we got."

Coughlin made the Giants wait for him. It turned out to be worth it. For both of them.■

THE GIANTS' SHOCKING SUPER SEASON

OUT OF THE BLUE.

NFC CHAMPIONSHIP
GIANTS 20 | 49ERS 17

ONCE ON THE BRINK OF COLLAPSE, THE GIANTS ARE ON THE VERGE OF HISTORY

BY RALPH VACCHIANO

Lawrence Tynes came running off the field after another overtime field goal, his index finger high in the misty air and pointing straight to another Super Bowl.

It all seemed so deliriously familiar to the erupting Giants on the sideline, who once again await the New England Patriots after a 20-17 overtime victory on Sunday night to advance to Super Bowl XLVI.

Even Tom Coughlin admitted resisting comparisons to the Giants' Super Bowl victory four years ago over the Pats is now futile, and there's no avoiding comparisons to the Giants' glorious past. These Giants, once on the brink of a "historical" collapse, are now on the verge of history.

"It is kind of eerie," said defensive end Justin Tuck. "We tried to downplay it all along, but I'd be lying to you if I said it didn't feel like 2007."

"It's pretty similar," added Giants co-owner John Mara. "Let's hope it stays that way."

They'll have a chance to make sure it does on Feb. 5 in Indianapolis when the Giants (12-7) face the AFC champion Patriots in a rematch of Super Bowl XLII - one of the greatest Super Bowls in history. And just like they did four years ago, they set that up that showdown with an overtime field goal by Tynes on the road.

This one was from 31 yards, 7:06 into the extra session, on the slick field at Candlestick Park. It came at the end of what Coughlin called "a classic football game that seemed like no one was going to put themselves in position to win."

Until somebody did.

Above: Giants fans celebrate the win at Salty Dog. *Ken Murray | Daily News*

Left: Kicker Lawrence Tynes watches his game-winning field goal sail through the uprights en route to the Super Bowl in Indianapolis. *Ron Antonelli | Daily News*

That somebody was rookie line-backer Jacquian Williams, who reached out and stripped the ball from 49ers punt returner Kyle Williams, who was filling in for the injured Ted Ginn, and immediately put the Giants inside Tynes' range. Kyle Williams had already muffed a punt in the fourth quarter, setting up the Giants' go-ahead touchdown. Then he did it again in overtime when Devin Thomas, who also recovered the previous muffed punt, recovered at the 49ers 24.

Five plays later, holder Steve Weatherford dug out Zak DeOssie's low snap and Tynes kicked it through the San Francisco mist.

"I blacked out, so I don't remember anything," Weatherford said. "But I do remember that ball going through the pipes."

That kick was the culmination of a brutal game that was exactly the "bloodbath" that Chris Canty predicted it would be. It began on a wet field in a driving rain that caused early trouble for both offenses. Eli Manning eventually found his groove, completing 32 of 58 passes for 316 yards and two touchdowns, while getting credit for his sixth fourth-quarter comeback of the year.

It was 49ers quarterback Alex Smith who struck first, on a 73-yard touchdown in the first quarter to tight end Vernon Davis who flew right by Giants safety Antrel Rolle. The Giants, riding the hot hand of Victor Cruz (10 catches, 142 yards) answered when a six-yard touchdown pass to tight end Bear Pascoe, and even had a 10-7 halftime lead when Tynes hit a 31-yard field goal at the end of the first half.

Right: Jason Pierre-Paul, left, and Justin Tuck, right, combine to sack San Francisco 49ers quarterback Alex Smith. *Ron Antonelli | Daily News*

OUT OF THE BLUE.

THE GIANTS' SHOCKING SUPER SEASON

Above: Little used Bear Pascoe comes up big with a second-quarter touchdown for the Giants. *Ron Antonelli | Daily News*
Right: Pascoe has reason to celebrate the Giants' first score in the NFC Championship Game.
Andrew Theodorakis | Daily News

In the second half, the 49ers seemed to be in control after Smith (12 for 26, 196 yards) again hit Davis (3-112-2), this time for a 28-yard touchdown late in the third. But then Kyle Williams made his first mistake, letting the ball bounce off his knee when he was trying to avoid a punt. Thomas recovered that one, too, giving the Giants the ball at the 49ers 29.

That set up Manning's 17-yard touchdown pass to Mario Manningham with 8:34 left in regulation, which at the time looked like it might turn out to be the game-winning score. But David Akers hit a 25-yard field goal with 5:39 remaining and the game ended up in overtime.

From there, both defenses turned up their games. The Giants' offense even stalled twice in overtime. Manning couldn't get anything going against the 49ers' fierce pass rush.

"(I was) just trying to be patient, that's kind of what I kept telling myself," he said. "Don't give them anything. Don't force anything. Guys never quit. They kept fighting, kept battling, no matter what the circumstances were. I think everyone knew we were going to get a chance to win this football game. Something was going to happen."

Something did with 9:32 remaining when Jacquian Williams forced the fumble that set up Tynes' kick, and just like that, 2007 was happening all over again. The Giants, once again the "Road Warriors" were on their way back to the Super Bowl, against the team they beat in such classic fashion in Glendale, Ariz. in Feb., 2008.

"I tried to fight it," Coughlin said. "I'm sitting in there and Osi (Umenyiora) is just smiling at me, saying 'Do you realize how this is coming down?' It's scary."

"It's amazing," Tynes added. "I had dreams about this last night."

For the second time in five seasons, those dreams incredibly came true.■

OUT OF THE BLUE.

BY MIKE LUPICA

SO THE GIANTS HAVE done it again now, out of the stars, made it back through another overtime and into a Super Bowl. Lawrence Tynes has kicked another overtime field goal, this time at old Candlestick Park, kicked them to a rematch in Indianapolis with Brady and Belichick and the Patriots. So the Giants go back to the big game, go back because of big defense and big luck Sunday night, go all the way to Indy from 7-7 in the regular season. Were they lucky Sunday night at old Candlestick? You know they were. Sometimes you need some luck to go with the magic.

It was 20-17 this time, Tynes getting the chance in overtime because a kid named Kyle Williams, the Bill Buckner of this game. Williams had a Steve Weatherford punt bounce off his knee in the fourth quarter, setting up the touchdown that briefly put the

Giants ahead this time. Then he fumbled one away to Devin Thomas in overtime that was the same as having his team's season go through his hands.

An overtime championship game for the Giants. Again. Nobody had ever had two of those, until Tom Coughlin's Giants, who came from nowhere to this one, who had that 7-7 record, and have now won five in a row from there, gone from nowhere to Indy.

When it was over Sunday, when there was a chance for Coughlin to have a quiet moment in the Giants locker room, he was sitting next to Osi Umenyiora, who turned to his coach and said, "Do you believe how all this is going down?"

Coughlin's Giants won it all from 10-6 four years ago. They try to do it from 9-7 this time. But here they are, here are the Giants again, back to being the biggest game in town, and in Jersey, and everywhere there are people who

Above: Jason Pierre-Paul, left, and Justin Tuck dance over San Francisco quarterback Alex Smith, who they sacked three times. *Ron Antonelli | Daily News*

OUT OF THE BLUE:

grew up loving this team, starting with the ones who go all the way back to the Polo Grounds.

Eli Manning threw it 58 times at old Candlestick Park Sunday night, completed 32, threw two touchdown passes, one a bullet to Mario Manningham after that punt bounced off poor Kyle Williams' knee when Williams shouldn't have been near that ball, at a time when the 49ers defense was beating up Eli Manning but good.

But Eli Manning didn't pick the Giants up and carry them to Indy Sunday the way he has carried them for so much of this amazing season. He had chances to win the game at the end of regulation, oh man did he, but could not, mostly because he was spending too much time picking himself off the ground.

Eli got the ball first in overtime and the Giants had to punt it and got it again and the Giants had to punt it away. And that is a way of telling you that the Giants go to the Super Bowl because of defense out of their past. Because they gave up two big plays — two touchdown drives for San Francisco that didn't last two minutes, total — and gave Alex Smith and the 49ers nothing the rest of the day and night in San Francisco.

The Giants go to another Super Bowl because even when one score could have cost them their season, when they had to keep punting the ball away, it was just one three-and-out after another for the other team, the guys on the Giants defense making you believe that the 49ers could play until Monday morning and not get another score off them.

Left: Brandon Jacobs is fired up for the start of the second half as the Giants hold a slim 10-7 lead at intermission.
Ron Antonelli | Daily News

THE GIANTS' SHOCKING SUPER SEASON

Above: Two of the Giants' heroes enjoy the moment as Eli Manning, right, slaps five with kicker Lawrence Tynes after the victory. *Ron Antonelli* | *Daily News*

"So many big stops," Eli Manning said in the interview room. "So much pressure."

Eli was at the podium and Tom Coughlin, who gets another dream run like this, was in the back of the room, waiting to go up to the front of the room himself.

Coughlin said in a quiet voice, "Did they even get a third-down conversion?"

And somebody said, "One, coach. They got one."

This wasn't Tom Brady they were facing, not yet. Wasn't Aaron Rodgers at Lambeau last week. This was Alex Smith, who looked more and more like a scared, rattled, overmatched kid the longer the game went.

Did Smith's team get bad breaks? The worst. Did they get a terrible whistle on what should have been an Ahmad Bradshaw fumble in the fourth quarter, one that would have set up a David Akers field goal at least? The 49ers got a terrible whistle, when it was clear Bradshaw hadn't been stopped. Sometimes when things start going your way, everything does, making you believe the whole thing really is in the stars again.

With five minutes left, the Giants punted. Smith got sacked by Osi and Mathias Kiwanuka on third down. Giants had to punt again. Smith threw three shaky incompletions in a row. Three and out, three and out. The

Score by Quarters	1	2	3	4	OT	Final
Giants	0	10	0	7	3	20
San Francisco	7	0	7	3	0	17

OUT OF THE BLUE:

49ers got the ball with 19 seconds left in regulation. Went nowhere. Three and out in the overtime and then the fumble from Williams and Tynes' overtime kick four years after the first one and the rematch with the Patriots, this time in Indianapolis, the Giants trying to win their fourth Super Bowl, which would merely put them two behind the Steelers and one behind the 49ers and Cowboys, and even with the Green Bay Packers.

Now Tom Coughlin was at the podium, trying to explain how he and his team had gotten to this moment from 7-7, another great moment for him and his players and his organization and his fans, maybe the best there are anywhere. Finally someone asked him about the comparisons between what happened four years ago and what is happening now and a great football coach said, "I'm trying to fight it."

No need, because of the fight in his team. New magic now to go with old magic. They give us 99-yard touchdowns and Hail Mary passes and a ball off a knee and a fumble in overtime and even a good whistle at the best possible time. Sometimes you need luck to go with the magic, especially when you come from nowhere and end up in another Super Bowl, carrying the rest of us along with you.∎

Above: Hakeem Nicks knows he can read all about the Giants' win in New York's hometown paper, the Daily News. *Ron Antonelli | Daily News*

SCORING SUMMARY

FIRST QUARTER
49ERS – V.Davis 73 pass from Ale.Smith (Akers kick), 7:11. .

SECOND QUARTER
GIANTS – Pascoe 6 pass from Manning (Tynes kick), 11:15.
GIANTS – FG Tynes 31, :02.

THIRD QUARTER
49ERS – V.Davis 28 pass from Ale.Smith (Akers kick), 5:18.

FOURTH QUARTER
GIANTS – Manningham 17 pass from Manning (Tynes kick), 8:34.
49ERS – FG Akers 25, 5:39.

OVERTIME
GIANTS – FG Tynes 31, 7:06.

SCORING SUMMARY

	GIANTS	SF
First downs	20	15
Total Net Yards	352	328
Rushes-yards	26-85	28-150
Passing	267	178
Punt Returns	6-55	8-70
Kickoff Returns	1-17	4-100
Interceptions Ret.	0-0	0-0
Comp-Att-Int	32-58-0	12-26-0
Sacked-Yards Lost	6-49	3-18
Punts	12-46.4	10-45.5
Fumbles-Lost	1-0	4-2
Penalties-Yards	9-60	6-50
Time of Possession	39:36	28:18

Attendance — 69,732

INDIVIDUAL STATISTICS

RUSHING
Giants — Bradshaw 20-74, Jacobs 5-13, Manning 1-(minus 2).
San Francisco — Gore 16-74, Ale.Smith 6-42, Hunter 4-31, Dixon 2-3.

PASSING
Giants — Manning 32-58-0-316.
San Francisco — Ale.Smith 12-26-0-196.

RECEIVING
Giants — Cruz 10-142, Bradshaw 6-52, Nicks 5-55, Beckum 4-16, Hynoski 3-20, Jacobs 2-8, Manningham 1-17, Pascoe 1-6.
San Francisco — Gore 6-45, V.Davis 3-112, Walker 2-36, Crabtree 1-3.

GAME STATS
JANUARY 22, 2012

GIANTS ARE

Mario Manningham makes acrobatic catch along the sideline, giving Giants great field position on game-winning drive. *Corey Sipkin | Daily News*

OUT OF THE BLUE

OUT OF THE BLUE.

SUPER BOWL
GIANTS 21 | PATRIOTS 17

IT'S A REPEAT PERFORMANCE FOR GIANTS AS MVP ELI PLAYS ROLE OF SUPERMANN II

BY RALPH VACCHIANO

Four years ago, John Mara stood on a podium in a swirl of confetti after witnessing what he called "the greatest victory in the history of this franchise." He was sure it was a once-in-a-lifetime moment.

Then, on Sunday night, it happened all over again.

History repeated itself in incredible fashion as the Giants rode another amazing fourth-quarter comeback by Eli Manning to win their second Super Bowl championship in four years. They beat the New England Patriots, again, in Super Bowl XLVI on an Ahmad Bradshaw touchdown with 57 seconds remaining, this time 21-17.

Then they withstood a final, desperate pass by Tom Brady, again, to hang on to a heart-stopping victory.

"To get one Super Bowl win in the manner that we got it four years ago usually lasts a whole career," Mara said from under another storm of confetti. "But to get two of these? It is beyond description. It really is."

Getting two in five seasons against the same rivals — a team with three Super Bowl rings of its own — is amazing enough, but they did it by nearly duplicated their miraculous championship run of 2007, right down to the final, nervewracking drive. This time they got the ball back at their own 12 with 3:46 remaining, trailing 17-15 and needing only a field goal to pull off the miracle.

They started fast, with a 38-yard pass down the sidelines to Mario Manningham, who made the highlight-reel catch at midfield by leaping and just barely getting his feet in bounds. Manning —

Above: New Yorkers from the Bronx and Long Island made the trek to Indianapolis to cheer on their beloved Giants.
Robert Sabo | Daily News

Left: The Giants take the field before beating the Patriots in the Super Bowl for the second time in four years.
Corey Sipkin | Daily News

OUT OF THE BLUE.

who set a Super Bowl record by completing his first nine passes and was named the MVP again for his stellar 30-for-40, 296-yard performance - completed four of his next five passes before the Pats let Bradshaw score on a 6-yard run with less than a minute to go.

Then the Giants defense took the field, thinking, as safety Kenny Phillips said, "Don't blow it. Just don't blow it." This time Brady — who set a Super Bowl record with 16 straight completions and finished 27 for 41 for 276 yards — had 22 seconds more than he had in Super Bowl XLII. And he nearly pulled off the biggest miracle of all when he fired a 49-yard Hail Mary pass into the end zone on the final play of the game.

Of the time ball was in the air, Mara said, "I couldn't breathe. That would've been a horrible way to lose the game." But Phillips leaped and knocked the ball away the Patriots' Aaron Hernandez. New England's injured tight end Rob Gronkowski lunged for the batted pass but it proved out of reach. The celebration was suddenly under way.

That Manning would lead the decisive drive was fitting, considering this was the seventh time he led the Giants back from a fourth-quarter deficit this season. But first, the Giants had to duck several potential disasters. The first came when the Patriots scored on the final drive of the first half and the opening series of the second to take what seemed like a commanding 17-9 lead.

"That could've sucked the momentum right out of us," Manning said. But they still had Tom Coughlin's halftime words

Left: Brandon Jacobs powers his way to 72 yards against New England.
Robert Sabo | Daily News

113

Above: Justin Tuck pressures Tom Brady forcing an intentional grounding call and a safety for Giants. *Ron Antonelli | Daily News*

Right: Justin Tuck goes through his post-sack ritual after bringing down Tom Brady. *Andrew Theodorakis | Daily News*

ringing in their ears. "When we got in at half-time I said, 'We can play better than this, guys. We're better than this,' " Coughlin said. "Everybody agreed."

First they chipped away with two Lawrence Tynes field goals to pull within 17-15. Then they escaped disaster when linebacker Chase Blackburn - only re-signed by the Giants in late November - boxed out Gronkowski deep in Giants territory and intercepted a Brady pass. Two plays later, guard Chris Snee dived on fumble by Bradshaw at the Giants' 11.

Then, with four minutes left, Brady had a wide-open Wes Welker deep in Giants territory, but the slightly high pass high bounced off the receivers' usually sure hands.

That set the stage, again, for Manning. And they knew what was going to happen next.

"It was almost relaxing, crazy as that sounds," said Justin Tuck. "I was smiling on the sidelines. We were like, 'We've been here before.' "

"It's Eli Manning," added Dave Tollefson. "What did you expect?"

Nobody expected this, not from a team that looked in August like it was rebuilding and then was on the brink of elimination with a 7-7 record and two games to go. Just like they did in 2007, though, they spent the next six weeks on a run for the ages.

By the time they got to the Super Bowl the feeling was so familiar they just knew they were about to win it all.

"We proved everyone wrong with our actions," said left tackle David Diehl. "It wasn't about what we said. It was what we did."

OUT OF THE BLUE

OUT OF THE BLUE.

What they will do now is take the trip to the White House they were chanting for in their post-game locker room, as well as the parade down the Canyon of Heroes they predicted they would get.

"No one can take this away from us, no matter what," added Antrel Rolle. "They can say whatever they want to say. They can put us down. They can say we got lucky. We know we're going to hear it all.

"But at the end of the day, we are the champions."

Again.■

Left: Young Victor Cruz and Giants fan will remember this game for the rest of his life. *Robert Sabo | Daily News*

Below: Salsa King Victor Cruz has some dancing to do in the end zone at the Super Bowl. *Howard Simmons | Daily News*

Opposite Page: Victor Cruz continues his amazing season by hauling in first TD of the Super Bowl. *Ron Antonelli | Daily News*

Ahmad Bradshaw runs to daylight as his offensive line clears the way.   *Howard Simmons | Daily News*

OUT OF THE BLUE.

BY MIKE LUPICA

THIS WAS THE NIGHT, in the second Super Bowl against the Patriots, the second time he won the game for his team in the last minute of a Super Bowl, that Eli Manning made it all official, that he is not just one of the great clutch quarterbacks in the history of his sport, but as great a clutch athlete as we have ever had in New York, in anything.

Nobody takes his team down the field and does it like this twice with an NFL championship on the line, not Johnny Unitas or Joe Montana or anybody. Only now Eli has. He has done it like this again and done it to the Patriots again, this time at Lucas Oil Stadium, this time handing the season to Ahmad Bradshaw at the end instead of throwing it to Plaxico Burress.

This time he started with three minutes and change left, instead of two minutes and change the way it was against the Patriots the last time. This time the throw to remember wasn't to David Tyree, it was 38 yards down the left sideline to Mario Manningham. Not as crazy a catch as Tyree made in Super Bowl 42. Just a much better throw from Eli Manning, from his own 12-yard line.

Now it was much later at Lucas Oil Stadium, and the Giants had won 21-17, and there was confetti everywhere and Jake Ballard, one of the receivers who caught balls from Eli all year long, was on a cart near the stage for the trophy presentation because he hurt his knee Sunday night against the Patriots. And Ballard was asked what it is in his quarterback's DNA that makes him become the best quarterback in the world and one of the best to ever play games like this when games like this are on the line.

"It's the Eli gene," Ballard said.

Much later than that, standing outside the

Above: Ahmad Bradshaw stiff-arms his way for extra yardage and also scores title-clinching TD.   *Ron Antonelli | Daily News*

OUT OF THE BLUE:

Giants locker room, Eli Manning's mother, Olivia, was asked what it was like when the Giants got the ball back Sunday night with 3:46 left and they were still trailing the Patriots 17-15, and she knew that once again her youngest son was being asked to bring the Giants from behind in the last minutes of the Super Bowl, and the family was in the barrel again, this time in the stadium where Peyton Manning had been such a great player.

"I have to tell you," she said, "I am always happy when the ball is in Eli's hands."

Archie Manning, a great quarterback who never got near a moment like this as a player, said, "And I'm pretty happy when the season is in his hands."

So much had happened in this game before Eli (30-for-40, 296 yards, one touchdown pass, second Super Bowl MVP) got the ball back on the 12, still down two. Tom Brady had completed 16 passes in a row during one stretch and the Patriots had scored 17 points in a row to go ahead 17-9. But with four minutes left, Wes Welker dropped a deep ball he should have caught, that might have set the Patriots up to put the game away. The Patriots had to punt finally from the Giants 44. First down for Eli on the 12. First play he threw one of the best pure, cold, money passes he will ever throw to Manningham. Who somehow kept his feet in bounds. Giants at the 50 now.

And you knew. You knew in Indy that it was happening to the Patriots again, that Eli was doing it to them again in this wonder-

Left: Ahmad Bradshaw approaches the end zone untouched and hesitates for a moment before finally falling forward for the winning touchdown.
Corey Sipkin| Daily News

Giant defenders leap to knock down Tom Brady's Hail Mary pass in end zone on game's final play.
Howard Simmons | Daily News

OUT OF THE BLUE

Above: Zak DeOssie shows the world who the Super Bowl champs are. *Ron Antonelli | Daily News*

ful Super Bowl, exactly what it was supposed to be, Giants-Patriots II feeling like Ali-Frazier III and making Justin Tuck say on the field, "I'm just glad we're Ali."

"That's a huge play right there," Eli said, on this night when he was the Super Bowl MVP for a second time. "When you're backed up, to get a 40-yard gain and get to the middle of the field ..."

He completed four more passes after that, two to Manningham and two to a great talent named Hakeem Nicks. Then Bradshaw ran into the end zone even though there was a crazy moment when you thought he might stop to run more clock. Then a desperation throw

from Brady was on the ground in the end zone, and the Giants really had come from 7-7 in December to win the fourth Super Bowl in the team's history.

Outside the Giants locker room, Osi Umenyiora was asked which one was sweeter, this one or the one four years ago, and he said, "This one. Know why? They said the one four years ago was a fluke. What are they gonna say now?"

They are going to say that the Giants have now given their fans, the best there are anywhere, the two best championship runs any New York team has ever given anybody in anything. And a season that started out with

SCORE BY QUARTERS	1	2	3	4	FINAL
Giants	9	0	6	6	21
New England	0	10	7	0	17

OUT OF THE BLUE.

Above: Giants QB Eli Manning pointed the way all season, his best as a professional. *Robert Sabo | Daily News*

the silly controversy of Eli saying he's an elite quarterback merely ends with Giants fans knowing they would not trade him for another elite quarterback or player in his sport, not Aaron Rodgers or Drew Brees or Brady or anybody.

Go find another quarterback who brought his team from behind twice in the last minute of a championship game like this. Oh, you get to do it once, the way Montana did against the Bengals in Miami one time. You do it the way Ben Roethlisberger did to the Cardinals in Tampa. You're not supposed to do it twice. Only now Eli Manning, who takes his place right now with Lawrence Taylor as one of the two Giants who will be remembered best.

"Maybe there is something in his DNA," Giants co-owner John Mara said. "Because the bigger the pressure, the cooler he is."

Mo Rivera closed out all those October games. Eli is a different kind of closer. He closes by coming from behind in the Super Bowl. Twice.

Other quarterbacks have more Super Bowls. Give him time. By now we know he doesn't need much. As great a clutch athlete as we've ever had here. Not just an elite quarterback last night. Best in the world. ■

SCORING SUMMARY

FIRST QUARTER
GIANTS – Team safety, 8:52.
GIANTS – Cruz 2 pass from Manning (Tynes kick), 3:24.

SECOND QUARTER
PATRIOTS – FG Gostkowski 29, 13:48.
PATRIOTS – Woodhead 4 pass from Brady (Gostkowski kick), :08.

THIRD QUARTER
PATRIOTS – Hernandez 12 pass from Brady (Gostkowski kick), 11:20.
GIANTS – FG Tynes 38, 6:43.
GIANTS – FG Tynes 33, :35.

FOURTH QUARTER
GIANTS – Bradshaw 6 run (run failed), :57.

SCORING SUMMARY

	GIANTS	NE
First downs	26	21
Total Net Yards	396	349
Rushes-yards	28-114	19-83
Passing	282	266
Punt Returns	1-10	0-0
Kickoff Returns	4-75	3-73
Interceptions Ret.	1-0	0-0
Comp-Att-Int	30-40-0	27-41-1
Sacked-Yards Lost	3-14	2-10
Punts	4-40.8	3-41.0
Fumbles-Lost	2-0	0-0
Penalties-Yards	4-24	5-28
Time of Possession	37:05	22:55

Attendance — 68,658

INDIVIDUAL STATISTICS

RUSHING
Giants — Bradshaw 17-72, Jacobs 9-37, Ware 1-6, Manning 1-(minus 1).
New England — Green-Ellis 10-44, Welker 2-21, Woodhead 7-18.

PASSING
Giants — Manning 30-40-0-296.
New England — Brady 27-41-1-276.

RECEIVING
Giants — Nicks 10-109, Manningham 5-73, Pascoe 4-33, Cruz 4-25, Bradshaw 2-19, Hynoski 2-19, Ballard 2-10, Ware 1-8.
New England — Hernandez 8-67, Welker 7-60, Woodhead 4-42, Branch 3-45, Gronkowski 2-26, Green-Ellis 2-15, Ochocinco 1-21.

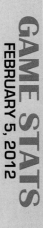

GAME STATS
FEBRUARY 5, 2012

OUT OF THE BLUE.

THE GIANTS' SHOCKING SUPER SEASON

Victor Cruz (80) and his Giants teammates share the Vince Lombardi trophy after dispatching the Patriots.
Howard Simmons | Daily News

OUT OF THE BLUE